Modelle für den neusprachlichen Unterricht Englisch

Herausgegeben von Dieter Langendorf

The American Dream

Myth and Reality in Contemporary America

by Gerhard Kirchner, Walter Kühnel and Harald Raykowski

Verlag Moritz Diesterweg

Frankfurt am Main · Berlin · München

ISBN 3-425-04471-0

Gesamtherstellung: Druckwerkstätten Koehler & Hennemann GmbH, Wiesbaden

Contents

GENERAL INTRODUCTION

America in the second half of the 20th century

The Americans, now into the first decade of their third century of national history, have undergone a strange transformation. Over the last twenty-odd years the color of the proverbial American Way of Life has changed from the old flamboyance of the Red-White-and-Blue to a dull gray. It is a stubborn, frustrating gray which, to friendly and hostile critics alike, the contemporary American citizen cannot shake. For the first time the polls indicate a nationwide fear of the future. Americans are afraid that "the future is not what it used to be". The majority is not silent but scared. Most Americans, the polls reveal, do not expect their children's life will be as good as their own.

Fear of the future is clearly "un-American". Probably no other nation in history has been so stimulated, enchanted, and propelled by a sense of and belief in the future. It is hardly an exaggeration to say that the United States were built on the conviction that somehow and sometime something better will happen to good Americans than has happened to man in other countries. Progress, the idea of inevitable progress, was the specifically American creed. For almost two hundred years, with the possible exceptions of the Civil War and the Depression, Americans moved forward through good times and bad with a sense that things would get even better. The next valley would be greener, the line on the graph would steadily climb, problems would be solved, technology would further improve the good life, American know-how would prevail, the right man and the right idea would be found to lead them into an even more enviable future. Had not the American people shown the way to perfection and had they not paved this road for others as well? Had not conditions of life been improved over each preceding decade, were not economic standards higher, scientific discoveries numerous, technological advances obvious? Did not education and social improvements promise further reduction, maybe even total elimination of poverty, ignorance and crime? The strong and optimistic belief in the future is the essence of the old American dream.

The last twenty-five years have almost reversed this belief. God's own country has lost its "morning eagerness". The deeply emotional attachment to the concept of progress has been weakened, if not completely dissolved. For a brief, shining moment Americans celebrated technology and its latest feat when they watched their astronauts walk on the moon. But how could this "great step forward" compete with the permanent problems of the cities? The golden hour did not stop pollution nor open new energy sources. The gas lines grew and the belief in technology and its promise of mastering the universe slowly but steadily waned. Vietnam shredded the comfortable notion of American military omnipotence. The news of the My Lai massacre shook the assumptions that America was "always the good guy", that her wars were fought "with God on our side". The smug selfrighteousness of American politics was revealed and the U.S. were pilloried in the United Nations.

The Bicentennial provided another shining but equally brief moment of celebration. It was brief because it could not obliterate Watergate, that indelible blot on the national record. Watergate proved that corruption and crime were not confined to back alleys nor reserved for little crooks. And how could one reconcile the conviction of the petty criminals with the immediate pardon of the former President by his successor? Politicians and businessmen were accused of and convicted for criminal activities which dwarfed the memory of Chicago's legendary mobsters. "Affairs" became scandals which, in turn, generated profound and pervasive distrust in government, eroded confidence in institutions, and dealt staggering blows to America's sense of her moral, economic, and political integrity.

The American economy suffered severe setbacks. The oil shortage gave Americans a first and second taste of limitations and energy dependency. Inflation picked the average American's pocket so relentlessly that the standard of living dropped sharply. Inflation and recession effectively challenged the comfortable American assurance of at least a bit more pie for practically everyone every year. Abroad the once mighty dollar staggered like a punch-drunk boxer on the brink of the final knock-out, and at home the greenback bought only half of what it had some five years ago. And, of course, when the staggering profit margins of Exxon and Texaco flickered across the TV-screen, such announcements hardly helped to restore faith in the system.

And Americans learned to witness hold-ups and muggings in broad daylight and fade quickly back into a side street rather than tell the police. Dramatic jumps in homicides were recorded. St. Louis, Atlanta, Houston, New York, and Dallas are competing for the dubious honor of being the murder capital of the U.S. The failure to curb capital crime has turned whole city districts into virtual war zones. Americans have learned to live with muggers, dope addicts, prostitutes, hit-men, and the rest of the urban scum. Chandler's bitter sarcasm has been amply vindicated by the American urban scene. The newspapers echo his words again and again: 'It is not funny that a man should be killed, but it is sometimes funny that he should be killed for so little, and that his death should be the coin of what we call civilization.'

The sense of a national purpose, the sense of community and cooperation

has been eroded by what a critic called “the war of the parts against the whole”. The country has been fragmented by the “Me-generation”, characterized by a new selfishness without guilt. Very understandably, most Americans have adopted the model which, they feel, economics and politics have set. If businessmen and politicians are taking what they can get, the average American says, I would be a fool not to take what I can get.
And, increasingly, frustrations are born out of a sense of helplessness. People are forced to cope with the situation at hand without seeing much choice. They feel the presence of forces which are beyond their reach. And for the most part, those forces are part of the system itself, the big machine which one cannot challenge directly. This helplessness, the irritation, and frustration create a sense of living in an age of perpetual crisis. America is no longer “the fresh green breast of the new world”, the land of the future. The American Dream is over. It has been shattered into a million jagged pieces. The idea of a land where milk and honey flows has been replaced by images of a 20th century wasteland. The notion of a “chosen people” has been replaced by the reality of a nation of middle-class hustlers.

Annotations

2 **decade** period of 10 years – 5 **flamboyance** brightness of colors, noticeable appearance – 5 **Red-White-and-Blue** the colors of the American flag – 7 **(opinion) poll** [pəul] G. Meinungsumfrage – 13 **enchanted** filled with delight – 13 **to propel** [-ˈ-] to drive forward, to motivate – 14 **United States / U.S.A.** AE. plural, BE singular – 19 **Civil War** between the North and the South, 1861–65 – 19 **Depression** period of unemployment in the 1930s – 21 **graph** G. Kurve(nbild) – 23 **to prevail** to be widespread – 24 **enviable** [ˈenviəbl] very desirable (cf. envy) – 29 **to eliminate** to get rid of – 33 **morning eagerness** (could be translated as) morgendlicher, jugendlicher Tatendrang – 38 **pollution** dirtying (of the environment) – 40 **to wane** to grow less – 41 **to shred** to tear into shreds or small pieces – 41 **omnipotence** [ɔmˈnipətəns] power over all things – 42 **My Lai** Vietnamese village whose population was massacred by US troops in 1968 – 44 **smug** too pleased with oneself – 45 **to pillory** G. anprangern – 46 **Bicentennial** [ˌbaisenˈteniəl] 200th anniversary of America’s independence in 1976 – 47 **to obliterate** to destroy – 47 **Watergate** political scandal in 1972, named from an apartment block in Washington, D.C., which led to President Nixon’s resignation – 48 **indelible** that cannot be rubbed out – 48 **blot** mark caused by ink spilt on paper; here: disgrace – 49 **crook** [-u-] thief – 50 **petty** (by comparison) unimportant – 53 **mobster** gangster – 55 **to erode** to wear away – 55 **staggering** causing one to walk unsteadily – 57 **setback** check to development – 59 **relentless** [-ˈ--] without pity – 63 **punch-drunk** (boxing) G. betäubt, groggy – 63 **on the brink of** very near (s.th. dangerous) – 64 **greenback** dollar note – 68 **hold-up** G. Überfall – 68 **to mug** to rob with violence – 70 **homicide** murder – 72 **to curb** to control – 72 **capital crime** G. Kapitalverbrechen – 73 **dope** (sl.) drug – 74 **hit-man** paid killer – 74 **scum** worthless evil people – 74 **Raymond Chandler** (1888–1959) Am. author of detective novels – 75 **sarcasm** bitter irony – 75 **to vindicate** to show or prove the truth, validity – 87 **to cope with** to deal successfully with s.th. – 92 **“fresh green breast . . .”** quotation from F. Scott Fitzgerald’s novel *The Great Gatsby* – 93 **jagged** with sharp edges – 94 **“. . . milk and honey . . .”** the promised land, cf. Exodus 3,8 – 96 **hustler** person who sells or obtains sth. by (deceitful) activity

A) Understanding the Text

1. The authors maintain that there has been a general belief in the future. What were the material and psychological reasons for this belief?
2. Point out the major disappointments which shattered this belief.
3. What role do crime and violence play in this process?
4. Explain the concept of the "Me-generation".
5. Why is the reality of poverty in America such an extremely disconcerting element?

B) Interpretation and Discussion

1. Discuss the hopes and beliefs which have created an "American Dream". To what degree does the American Dream differ from European aspirations?
2. Discuss the role of technology in the creation of a superior civilization. Do you believe that time- and labor-saving machinery sets free additional qualities in a human being? Or will technology suppress human dreams?
3. Violence is a phenomenon which America shares with the rest of the world. Discuss the different reasons for violent behavior in different countries.

C) Creative Writing

Write an essay on what the U.S.A. mean to you.
What are your views of America's major problems and advantages?

moral crisis

I. The American Dream: Myth and Reality

Annotation

Mac (sl.) used for addressing a man whose name is not known; fellow – **jagged** ['dʒægid] with sharp, uneven edges – **hustler** ['hʌslə] person who sells or obtains s.th. by deceitful activity

1. What Is Happening To the American Dream?

by Jack Anderson

He is a self-described muckraker, a columnist and now a TV personality. But Jack Anderson is first a reporter, one who has become deeply concerned with what he considers to be a full-scale moral crisis in the United States. Here is his searing assessment.

Future historians may look back on America, as Edward Gibbon did on ancient Rome, as a nation that fell of its own excesses. There are signs of rot on all sides, signs that the nation's ideals are being sapped by permissive immorality.

The phrase is not used here in any prissy, holier-than-thou sense. It refers to those basic values and virtues, or the lack of them, that have determined historically whether a nation holds together and transmits to its children the sources of its strength and vitality.

A survey of U.S. leaders, ranging from octogenarian labor chief George Meany to nonconformist civil rights leader Jesse Jackson, attests to the growing concern over the nation's moral fiber and what it may portend. Let's examine some of the questions tearing at the soul of America:

Will the American Way parallel the Decline and Fall of the Roman Empire?

Not to take anything away from the decadence of past generations, the America of the 1970's is in a class by itself. Never before has so large a share of the population indulged in an orgy of self-pampering, overdosing, loafing, sponging, splurging, cheating, shoplifting, looting, philandering, even murdering. That's what the statistics show.

Or consider these glimpses of the American scene: child prostitutes and Lolita-age models pictured in nudie magazines... Charles Manson and his murderous harem glorified into a pop cult... wife-swapping in the suburbs and gay bars in the cities... businessmen spending their lunch hours watching bottomless go-go dancers... New York's Times Square, the most visible acre of America, a national eyesore... Needle Park for the junkies and Watergate for the White House... high jinks on Capitol Hill.

"We're in a civilizational crisis," declares the Rev. Jesse Jackson. He cites the bitterly divisive Vietnam War, the assassination of one President and the disgrace of another, the years of civil strife in the streets. "Americans have been traumatized by distrust," he says. "This generation of adults hasn't gained the confidence of the current generation of youth. We've got too many doctors who put personal wealth ahead of the public health, too many lawyers who are more concerned with judgeships than justice. The result has been an ethical collapse."

From American Enterprise Institute, a Washington think tank, Robert Woodson echoes: "We've definitely got an ethical crisis in the nation." He blames the bureaucrats for the national failure to cope with the conditions that breed decaying morals. Dr. Nathan Glazer, a Harvard sociology professor, places heavy blame on television for the decline in traditional social and moral values.

But historian Arthur Schlesinger Jr., a member of the late John F. Kennedy's inner circle, takes exception. "The yearnings of today's society aren't any different from those of other periods in our nation's history," he contends. Violence and lawlessness were much worse in New York City in the late 18th century, he says, adding, "There's no inexorable moral decline in America. We're in a period of moral growth, not decay." The problem, he suggests, may be that the American people are feeling too much guilt. "Public sensitivity to corrupt behavior is greater than ever before," he says. "Maybe too great."

Have the nation's moral standards sunk too low? Where is "responsible society"?

More disturbing than mass misbehavior is its acceptance by what used to be called responsible society. This group could be counted on, in ways subtle and harsh, to repress or at least isolate the more antisocial vices. But now these vices have infiltrated and neutralized almost every segment of American society.

Vices that had been confined to the back streets are now on open display. The once-intolerable is now tolerated, excused away, sympathized with, even encouraged. Our institutions are becoming impotent before the moral erosion.

Judges, in the face of mass violations, are unable to enforce our laws against prostitution, gambling, homosexual acts, illegal strikes against the public. Contemporary society ignores the laws, begins to repeal them and declares it a victory for enlightenment.

President Carter's pastor, Dr. Charles Trentham, laments: "There's so little remorse shown today by those who violate the social and sexual mores. The bad in our society is getting worse."

Yet at the same time, he believes, "the good is getting better. The pendulum is swinging back." Agrees Stanford sociology professor Seymour Lipset: "Most people during this time of social and moral turmoil have adhered to conventional morality."

And former FBI chief Clarence Kelley told me "there are increasing indications that America's crime rate may be lower in the future."

Has the growing what's-in-it-for-me attitude cost America its industrial supremacy?

Many Europeans feel that "America has slacked off." The impression is spreading that "Americans are no longer willing to work." A recent survey concludes that more than 2 million able-bodied men spend their days puttering around the house and have no intention of ever going to work. Some are supported by women, others by the taxpayers. They feel no stigma, because in widening circles it is no longer considered poor form to let oneself be supported by another's labor and sacrifice.

The declining work ethic is costing our nation the economic supremacy in the world. Absenteeism and substandard performances, particularly among young workers, is a major problem. Businesses that once were able to compensate for poor worker performance by selling better and better machines can't do it now because profits are too low, taxes are too high and investors are scared off. Several large American industries are no longer fully competitive with foreign rivals.

The price paid for shabby workmanship is alarming. Worse, thefts by employees are today a major cost of doing business. The American worker, once by far the world leader in productivity, has now fallen far down the scale.

In behalf of the workers, George Meany told my office: "The immorality of massive unemployment, with the suffering and hardship it creates, still has not been met."

If there is a bright spot in this picture, it is the scattered signs of grassroots resistance to the new morality. Increasingly, college students have begun to abandon fake courses in favor of tougher ones that will lead to professions. Educators who turned their backs and let millions of corridor-roaming students pass through their schools without learning to read and write are being inundated by public demands for discipline and "back to basics." When a New York Times column made excuses for the looters in the summer blackout, a storm of protesting letters poured in. Politicians are running scared from demands of militants to let homosexuals come out of hiding; the rank and file of voters are saying: "Keep it private." While the federal judiciary stumbles around with pornography, local citizens groups and prosecutors are beginning to raise a rumpus.

A Wisconsin judge who spoke callously of rape was promptly booted out by voters. Religions that "stand for something" in personal morals seem to be enjoying phenomenal growth, and sexual promiscuity has somewhat declined among the young.

How strong is public reaction?

The anti-permissive public reaction that is roaring in upon our legislators, bureaucrats, jurists, psychiatrists and academicians is only beginning to have its effect. The traditionalist majority seems to be saying that, in our effort to correct social abuses and make life easier, we have gone too far in stripping away incentives to do right and punishments for doing wrong. They say that by eliminating tests that must be passed, responsibilities that must be borne and penalties that must be paid, society has encouraged the rise of the incompetent, the weak and the trivial.

Just how deep the wellsprings of moral revival run, no one knows. At stake is whether Americans will prove a great and enduring people or a third-rate bunch who lucked onto a first-rate continent and prospered for a while until they squandered their heritage.

Only a few of our forebears were the religious refugees and scrupulous specimens we read about as children. Most of us are descended from down-on-their-luck types – debtors, ex-jailbirds and rejects who came here or were exiled here for one last chance.

For 300 years America was a miracle to all the world, not because it showed what an elite could do but rather what cast-offs can do given a little elbow room and a chance to breathe freely. Here, challenge unleashed dormant energy; opportunity awakened sleeping talents; danger and hardship brought forth unsuspected courage and endurance; freedom enabled people to grow to full stature.

Somehow our post-industrial society, if it is to remain relatively free, productive and stable, must find ways to again make real the challenge of achievement, the penalty of failure, the reward for striving and the liberating energy that today is more and more stultified.

Only if we can do this can the old visions be made new again.

From: *Parade (Times-News),* March 19, 1978, pp. 4–7

Annotations

3 **muckraker** journalist who exposes misconduct of prominent people – 6 **searing assessment** [ˈsiəriŋ] (approximately) G. vernichtendes Urteil – 8 **Edward Gibbon** (1737–1794) English historian, wrote *The Decline and Fall of the Roman Empire* – 9 **rot** decay – 10 **to sap** to weaken or destroy – 10 **permissive** over-tolerant, esp. in sexual matters – 12 **prissy** G. zimperlich – 12 **holier-than-thou** G. frömmelnd, pharisäisch – 16 **octogenarian** [ˌɔktəudʒiˈnɛəriən] person between 80 and 89 – 17 **to attest to** to give proof of – 18 **moral fiber** (BE-re) moral quality – 18 **to portend** G. deuten auf (Zukünftiges) – 23 **orgy** [ˈɔːdʒi] G. Orgie – 23 **to pamper** to treat too kindly – 23 **to loaf** to waste time, esp. by not working when one should – 24 **to sponge** [spʌndʒ] G. schmarotzen – 24 **to splurge** to spend more money than one can usually afford – 24 **to shoplift** to steal from a shop – 24 **to philander** [fiˈlændə] (of a man) to amuse o.s. by making love to women, with no serious intentions – 27 **nudie magazine** [ˈnjuːdi ˈmægəziːn] magazine showing women without clothes – 27 **Charles Manson** fanatic leader of a Californian gang of murderers in the late 1960s – 28 **to glorify** to make s.th. inferior seem more splendid than it really is – 28 **to swap** [swɔp] (coll.) to exchange – 29 **gay** homosexual – 30 **bottomless** (cf. topless) wearing no panties – 30 **go-go dancer** night-club dancer – 31 **eyesore** s.th. ugly to look at – 31 **junkie** drug addict – 32 **high jinks** wild fun – 33 **to cite** to mention as an example – 34 **divisive** [diˈvaisiv] causing disunity – 34 **assassination** murder for political reasons – 35 **strife** trouble between people – 36 **trauma** [ˈtrɔːmə] mental shock – 39 **judgeship** office, status of a judge – 41 **think tank** G. Komitee von Experten – 48 **to take exception** to object – 48 **yearning** [ˈjəːniŋ] strong desire – 49 **to contend** to claim – 51 **inexorable** [inˈegzərəbl] G. unerbittlich – 61 **to infiltrate** G. unterwandern, durchsetzen – 68 **gambling** G. Glücksspiel – 69 **to repeal (a law)** to put an official end to – 70 **enlightenment** G. Aufklärung – 72 **remorse** regret for having done wrong – 72 **mores** [ˈmɔːreiz] moral customs and standards – 74 **pendulum** [ˈpendʒuləm] G. Pendel – 76 **turmoil** confusion and excitement – 76 **to adhere to** to be faithful to – 81 **supremacy** power – 82 **to slack off** to become less active – 85 **to putter around** (BE potter) to move aimlessly – 87 **stigma** (here:) shame – 90 **absenteeism** regular absence from work – 94 **competitive** G. konkurrenzfähig – 103 **grass roots** the ordinary people, not the ones in power – 105 **fake** (here:) not serious – 106 **to roam** to wander about aimlessly – 108 **to inundate** to flood – 109 **looter** G. Plünderer – 110 **blackout** G. Stromausfall – 112 **rank and file** the common (people etc.) – 113 **judiciary** G. Justiz – 114 **rumpus** noisy disagreement – 115 **callous** unfeeling – 115 **to boot out** to

dismiss - 117 **promiscuity** state of not being limited to one sexual partner - 124 **incentive** encouragement - 128 **wellspring** source - 130 **bunch** (sl.) group - 130 **to luck onto** to find by chance - 131 **squander** G. verschleudern - 131 **heritage** [ˈheritidʒ] G. Erbe - 132 **forebear** forefather, ancestor - 133 **down on one's luck** without money - 134 **jailbird** G. Zuchthäusler - 134 **reject** [ˈri:-], **cast-off** G. Ausgestoßener - 138 **to unleash** [ʌnˈli:ʃ] to set free - 138 **dormant** G. schlummernd, verborgen - 145 **to stultify** to spoil, weaken, make appear foolish

A) Understanding the Text

1. What symptoms does Anderson cite to prove the decadence of American society?
2. Compare the different views of the Rev. J. Jackson, R. Woodson, Dr. N. Glazer and A. Schlesinger Jr. of the causes for this decline.
3. How does Anderson describe the modern work ethic of his country?
4. Compare Anderson's attitude towards the problem of unemployment with that of George Meany, former president of the AFL-CIO (American Federation of Labor - Congress of Industrial Organizations, i.e. the central organization of American trade-unions).
5. Explain what Anderson means by "grassroots resistance", the phenomenon that makes him feel optimistic about the future of America.
6. How does he see the origins of Americans? What is his interpretation of the opportunities America once offered to people from all over the world?
7. What, to Anderson's mind, are the challenges which American society has to meet if it wants to remain free, productive and stable?

B) Interpretation and Discussion

1. To what extent are the phenomena and incidents that Anderson mentions in order to prove his theory of moral decline really representative of modern American society?
2. Discuss the different attitudes of Jackson, Woodson, Glazer and Schlesinger toward the causes of "immorality".
3. Anderson names unemployment as one of the major causes of social disorder. Whom does he blame for decreasing productivity - workers, economy, industry, politicians? What is your opinion of this problem?
4. Do you agree with the author's optimistic outlook on the role of the "traditional majority" in the battle against immorality, crime and disorder?
5. Would you consider Anderson's basic attitude as conservative or progressive? Substantiate your opinion by examining the text once again.

6. In the next to last passage, Anderson defines what he calls the American Dream in the headline of his essay. Can you explain this expression in your own words?
7. Discuss the pros and cons of a liberal attitude toward sexuality.

C) Language Work

1. Choose the word or phrase which is closest in meaning to the one in italics.

   a) Bigger organizations tend to be more *efficient.*
   i) powerful ii) effective iii) productive iv) wealthy

   b) Given the choice, most Americans choose fewer *product acquisitions.*
   i) purchases of goods ii) shopping opportunities iii) means of production iv) brands of products

   c) Most Americans are *absorbed with* the problems of daily life.
   i) worried about ii) occupied by iii) interested in iv) shocked at

   d) Americans *apparently* want less competition.
   i) probably ii) usually iii) definitely iv) possibly

2. Change the phrases and clauses in italics into a compound adjective, i.e. an adjective made up of a past participle joined to another word by a hyphen.

   Example: A hat *with a broad brim* = a *broad-brimmed* hat

   A firm *based in Detroit*
   A street *swept by the wind*
   Susan *with black eyes*
   A man *with long hair*
   A politician *who speaks well*
   A teacher *who has been trained in college*
   Shoes *which have rubber soles*

2. Face the flag

Face the flag of stars and bars
Of red and white and blue,
A flag that guarantees the rights
For men like me and you.

Face the flag, son! Read what's written there,
The history, the progress and the heritage we share.
Our flag reflects the past, son, but stands for so much more
And in this age of Aquarius, it still flies in the fore.

It leads the forward movement, shared by all mankind,
To learn... To love... To live with peace of mind;
To learn the mysteries of space, as well as those of earth
To love each man for what he is, regardless of his birth;
To live without the fear of reprisal for belief;
To ease the tensions of a world that cries out for relief.

Face the flag of stars and bars
Of red and white and blue,
A flag that guarantees the rights
For men like me and you.

Face the flag, son! Take a good long look.
What you're seeing now can't be found in a history book.
It's the present and the future, son. It's being written now
And you're the one to write it, but the flag can show you how.
Do you know what it stands for? What its makers meant?
To think... To speak... The privilege of dissent;
To think our leaders might be wrong... to stand and tell them so.
These are the things that other men under other flags will never know.
But responsibility... that's the cross that free men must bear
And if you don't accept that, the freedom isn't there.

Face the flag of stars and bars
Of red and white and blue,
A flag that guarantees the rights
For men like me and you.

Face the flag, son, and face reality.
Our strengths and our freedoms, are based in unity.
The flag is but a symbol, son, of the world's greatest nation
And as long as it keeps flying, there's cause for celebration.
So do what you've got to do, but always keep in mind
A lot of people believe in peace... but there are the others.
If we want to keep these freedoms, we may have to fight again.
God forbid, but if we do, let's always fight to win,
For the fate of a loser is futile and it's bare...
No love... No peace... just misery and despair.

Face the flag, son... and thank God it's still there.

From: John Wayne, *"America, Why I Love Her"*
Music: Billy Liebert
Words: Bill Ezell

Annotations

7 **heritage** [ˈheritidʒ] G. das Erbe – 9 **Age of Aquarius** [əˈkwɛəriəs] mythological age of freedom and brotherhood, celebrated in the hippie musical *Hair* (**Aquarius** G. Sternbild des Wassermanns) – 9 **in the fore** noticeable – 14 **reprisal** [riˈpraizl] punishment – 15 **tension** feeling of worry or pressure – 25 **dissent** [-ˈ-] difference of opinion – 42 **futile** [ˈfju:tail] useless

A) Understanding the Text

1. Which flag does John Wayne mean and how does he describe it?
2. Explain what the flag means to John Wayne.
3. How does John Wayne define "the forward movement" which is led by the country represented by this flag?
4. For John Wayne the flag is a symbol. A symbol of what?
5. In the last stanza Wayne explains what can be done to defend the values and virtues represented by the flag. Summarize this in your own words.

B) Interpretation and Discussion

1. How does John Wayne see the role and position of the USA among the nations of the world? Do you agree with him?
2. Wayne sings about "our flag", "our strenghts", "our freedoms". At the end he says: "If we want to keep these freedoms, we may have to fight again." Can you imagine who "the others" might be who don't believe in peace? What do you think of the distinction between those who believe in peace and those who don't?

3. Symbols mean different things to different people. If the Star-Spangled Banner means freedom, peace and democracy to a white American like John Wayne, what, do you think, could it mean to minorities like the Blacks and Indians?
4. How would you sum up the basic intention of this text by John Wayne, written in 1973 and released in 1974 (a time when the American political scene was characterized by the Vietnam War, the Watergate scandal and economic crises)?

Interpretation and Discussion

Inscribed in bronze on the pedestal of the Statue of Liberty, the American symbol of freedom, are these lines: "Give me your tired, your poor, your huddled masses yearning to breathe free."
Discuss the contrast between the situation presented in the cartoon and the promise expressed in the inscription.

"Give me your watch, your wallet, your credit cards . . . !"

From: *Punch,* Febr. 2, 1980

II. Violence and the Ghetto

Americans, certainly, have reason to inquire whether, in comparison with other advanced industrial nations, they are not a people of exceptional violence. The United States has a voluminous record of domestic violence, and the 60's and 70's have substantially added to this record. Riots and arson were, for some time, a summertime commonplace; the pictures of political assassinations shocked the whole nation: President John F. Kennedy, Martin Luther King, Robert F. Kennedy. The ritual murder-raids of the Manson gang made national headlines in 1969. Psychopathic cretins masquerading as "Son of Sam" or the "Hillside Strangler" killed literally dozens of people from New York to Los Angeles. The mass suicide of the People's Temple sect in Guyana in 1978 defies understanding. It is inconceivable to regard the persisting high level of crime and violence as a marginal problem and it is difficult not to interpret this turbulence as a symptom of a serious and general sickness of American society itself. The ghetto, the urban areas where socially, economically and racially discriminated people live, has seen the worst of this side of the American medal. Time and again have the sharp distinctions between the rich and the poor, the haves and have-nots, resulted in senseless but understandable violence.

Annotations

4 **domestic** of the house, home, or family; of one's own country – 5 **arson** G. Brandstiftung – 8 **raid** quick attack – 9 **cretin** [kri:tn] morally and intellectually inferior person – 9 **to masquerade** [ˌmæskəˈreid] G. sich maskieren oder ausgeben als – 10 **"Son of Sam", "Hillside Strangler"** notorious mass murderers of the recent past – 12 **inconceivable** [ˌinkənˈsi:vəbl] hard to believe; impossible – 12 **to defy** to offer difficulties that cannot be overcome – 13 **marginal** of small importance

Harlem

1. Male, Fair Hair, Dead on 123rd Street

The Negro detectives, Grave Digger Jones and Coffin Ed Johnson, were making their last round through Harlem in the old black Plymouth sedan with the unofficial tag, which they used as their official car. In the daytime it might have been recognized, but at night it was barely distinguishable from any number of other dented, dilapidated struggle buggies cherished by the citizens of Harlem, other than when they had to go somewhere in a hurry it went. But now they were idling along, west on 123rd Street, with the lights out as was their custom on dark side streets. The car scarcely made a sound; for all its dilapidated appearance the motor was ticking almost silently. It passed along practically unseen, like a ghostly vehicle floating in the dark, its occupants invisible.

This was due in part to the fact that both detectives were almost as dark as the night, and they were wearing lightweight black alpaca suits and black cotton shirts with the collars open. Whereas other people were in shirt sleeves on this hot night, they wore their suit coats to cover the big glinting nickel-plated thirty-eight calibre revolvers they wore in their shoulder slings. They could see in the dark streets like cats, but couldn't be seen, which was just as well because their presence might have discouraged the vice business in Harlem and put countless citizens on relief.

Actually they weren't concerned with prostitution or its feeder vices, unlicensed clubs, bottle peddlers, petit larceny, short con and steering. They had no use for pansies, but as long as they didn't hurt anyone, pansies could pansy all they pleased. They weren't arbiters of sex habits. There was no accounting for the sexual tastes of people. Just don't let anyone get hurt. If white citizens wished to come to Harlem for their kicks, they had to take the venereal risks and the risks of short con or having their money stolen. Their only duty was to protect them from violence.

They went down the side street without lights to surprise anyone in the act of maiming, mugging, rolling drunks, or committing homicide.

They knew the first people to turn on them if they tried to keep the white man out of Harlem after dark would be the whores themselves, the madams, the pimps, the proprietors of the late hour joints, most of whom were paying off some of their colleagues on the force.

For such a hot night, Harlem had been exceptionally peaceful. No riots, no murders, only a few cars stolen, which wasn't their business, and a few domestic cuttings. They were taking it easy.

'It's been a quiet night,' Coffin Ed said from his seat by the sidewalk.

'Better touch wood,' Grave Digger replied, lazily steering with one hand.

'There ain't any wood in this tin lizzie.'

'There's the baseball bat that man was beating his old lady with.'

'Hell, bats are made of plastic these days. Too bad we ain't got his head.'

'Lots of them around. Next one we come to I'll stop.'

'How about that one?'

Grave Digger looked ahead through the windscreen and saw the back of a black man in a black ensemble with a red fez stuck on his head. He knew the man hadn't seen them as yet nevertheless he was running as though he meant it. The man was carrying a pair of light gray pants over one arm with the legs blowing in the breeze as though they were running too, but a little faster.

'Look at that boy picking 'em up and laying 'em down like the earth was red-hot.'

'Reckon we ought to ask him?' Coffin Ed said.

'What for? To hear him lie? The white man who owned those pants ought to have kept them on.'

Coffin Ed chuckled. 'You said the next one we came to you'd stop.'

'Yeah, and you said it was quiet too. Let's keep it that way. What's unusual about a black brother stealing a whitey's pants who's laying up somewhere with a black whore?'

They were relaxed and indifferent. It wasn't their business to rescue the pants of a white man who was stupid enough to let them be stolen. They knew of too many cases where the white John went in the room and left his trousers draped over a chair by the door – with his money in it.

'The first thing to learn about whore chasing is what to do with your money while screwing.'

'That's simple,' Grave Digger said. 'Leave what you don't need at home.'

'And let your old lady find it? What's the difference?'

They let the fez-headed man get out of sight while they shot the bull. Suddenly Coffin Ed blurted, 'It ain't quiet no more.'

A bareheaded white man had materialized suddenly from the darkness into the dim pool of yellow light spilling from a street lamp, trying to run in the direction taken by the black man. But he staggered on wobbly legs as though drunk. They could see his legs plainly because he didn't wear any pants. In fact he didn't wear any underpants either and they could see his bare white ass beneath his white shirttail.

Grave Digger switched on the headlamps and the next instant he stepped on the accelerator. The car pulled to the curb beside the staggering man with the scream of tires on pavement, and both big double-jointed detectives emerged from opposite sides of the car like hoboes alighting from a moving freight. For an instant there was only the sound of flat feet slapping on concrete as they converged upon the tottering white man from fore and aft.

Coming up from the front side Grave Digger drew his torch. It was a rapid dangerous looking motion until the light hit the man's face. Grave Digger drew up sharp. Coffin Ed, coming from the rear, pinioned the white man's arms.

'Hold him steady,' Grave Digger said, fishing out his shield and turning the light on it. 'We're policemen. You're safe.'

Even while saying it he thought it was a stupid thing to say. The front of the white man's shirt was covered with blood. More blood spurted from the side of his throat where his jugular had been cut.

The white man shuddered convulsively and began sinking to the ground. Coffin Ed held him up. 'What's the matter with him?' he asked. He couldn't see from behind.

'Throat cut.'

The white man's mouth was clamped shut as though he were holding in his life. Blood spurted from the wound at every third or fourth heartbeat. Drops trickled from his nose. His eyes were beginning to glaze.

'Lay him on his back,' Grave Digger said.

Coffin Ed lowered the body full-length on its back down the dirty pavement. Both of them could see that life was going fast. He was not a pretty sight stretched out in the headlight glare. There was no chance of saving his life. That urgency had passed. Now there was a different urgency. It sounded in Grave Digger's voice as he bent over the dying man, thick, constricted, cottony dry:

'Quick! Quick! Who did it?'

The glazing eyes of the dying man gave no sign of comprehension, only the grim, clamped mouth tightened slightly.

Grave Digger bent closer to hear should the clamped lips open. Blood spurted from the man's cut throat into his face, suddenly nauseating him with its sweet, sickish scent. But he ignored it as he tried to hold the man on to life by his eyes.

'Quick!' Urgent, dry, compelling. 'A name? Give us a name!' His jaw muscles rippled over gritted teeth.

A last brief flicker of comprehension showed in the white man's eyes. For an infinitesimal instant the pupils contracted slightly. The man was making a tremendous effort to speak. The strain was visible in a slight tightening of the muscles of the face and neck.

'Who did it? Quick! A name!' Grave Digger hammered, his black face bloody and contorted.

The white man's tightly clamped lips trembled and suddenly opened, like a seldom used door. A liquid, gurgling sound came out, followed instantly by a gush of blood in which he drowned.

'"Jesus,"' Grave Digger echoed as he slowly straightened his bent figure. '"Jesus bastard!" What a thing to say.'

Coffin Ed's face was like a thundercloud. 'Jesus, Digger, Goddammit!' he flared. 'What you want him to say, Jesus hallelujah? The mother-raper got his throat cut for a black whore –'

'How you know it was a black whore who did it?'

'By whoever!'

'All right, let's call the precinct,' Grave Digger said thoughtfully, playing his flashlight over the dead man's body. 'Male, fair hair – blue eyes; jugular vein cut, dead on 123rd Street –' Glancing at his watch. '3:11 a.m.,' he recited.

Coffin Ed had hurried back to the car to get the precinct station on the radio. 'Without his pants,' he added.

'Later.'

While Coffin Ed was transmitting the essential facts over the radio-phone, colored people in various stages of undress began emerging from the black dark tenements alongside. Black women in terrycloth robes with their faces greased and their straightened hair done in small tight plaits like Topsy; brownskinned women with voluptuous breasts and broad buttocks wrapped in bright colored nylon, half-straight hair hanging loosely about their cushion-mouthed sleepy-eyed faces; high yellows in their silks and curlers. And the men, old, young, nappy headed, conk-haired, eyes full of sleep, faces lined where witches were riding them, mouths slack, wrapped in sheets, blankets, raincoats, or just soiled and wrinkled pajamas. Collecting in the street to see the dead man. Looking inexpressibly stupid in their morbid curiosity. A dead man was always good to see. It was reassuring to see somebody else dead. Generally the dead men were also colored. A white dead man was really something. Worth getting up any time of night. But no one asked who cut him. Nor why. Who was going to ask who cut a white man's throat in Harlem? Or why? Just look at him, baby. And feel good it ain't you. Look at that white mother-raper with his throat cut. You know what he was after....

Grave Digger turned towards the silent crowd collecting in the shadows. "Any of you know anything that might help?"

"H. Exodus Clay is the name of an undertaker," a brother said.

"Does this look like a time for that?"

"To me it does. When a man's dead you got to bury him."

From: Chester Himes, *Blind Man With A Pistol,* London, Panther Books, 1971

Annotations

4 **tag** (sl.) automobile number plate – 6 **struggle buggy** (sl.) automobile – 19 **vice** (here:) illegal doings, esp. prostitution – 20 **to put s.o. on relief** to put s.o. out of work **(relief** G. Wohlfahrtsunterstützung) – 21 **feeder vices** G. kriminelle Handlungen, die anderen Ungesetzlichkeiten Vorschub leisten – 22 **bottle peddler** (BE pedlar) G. fliegender Händler, der illegal Alkohol verkauft – 22 **petit** (or: **petty) larceny** ['peti 'lɑ:sni] (law) G. leichter Diebstahl – 22 **short con** (sl.) confidence game in a small way, G. kleine Betrügerei – 22 **steering** (sl.) directing people to a gambling casino etc., G. "Schleppen" – 23 **to have no use for** (coll.) to dislike – 26 **for kicks** (sl.) in order to get (amoral) pleasure or excitement – 27 **to take venereal risks** [vi'niəriəl] to risk getting venereal disease (G. Geschlechtskrankheit) – 30 **to mug** to assault, usually with intent to rob – 30 **to roll** (sl.) to rob (a drunk, sleeping, or unconscious person) – 34 **to pay s.o. off** (sl.) to give money to s.o. to prevent him from causing difficulties to o.s. (e.g. a protection gang) – 34 **force** i.e. police force – 37 **domestic cuttings** (could be translated as) G. häusliche Messerstechereien – 40 **tin lizzie** (sl.) originally in the 20's a Model T Ford, hence any motor car – 58 **to be laying up** (substandard for:) lying up – 62 **John** (sl.) man – 65 **to screw** (sl.) to have sexual intercourse – 68 **to shoot the bull** (sl.) to talk idly, to chat – 80 **freight** i.e. freight train – 84 **to draw up sharp** to stop abruptly – 86 **shield** (sl.) G. Polizeimarke – 90 **jugular (vein)** ['dʒʌgjulə vein] G. Halsschlagader – 115 **infinitesimal** [ˌinfini'tesəml] very small – 130 **precinct** ['pri:siŋ(k)t] (here:) police station – 138 **terrycloth** G. Frottee – 139 **plait** [pleit] (BE [plæt]) G. Zopf – 139 **Topsy** character in the book *Uncle Tom's Cabin* – 140 **voluptuous** of a woman: having a beautiful soft rounded body that excites sexual feeling – 140 **buttocks** the bottom (G. Hin-

tern) – 143 **nappy headed** kinky-haired, G. kraushaarig – 143 **conk-haired** with a hairstyle in which the (kinky) hair is straightened out and flattened down – 145 **to soil** to make dirty – 145 **pajamas** BE pyjamas [pəˈdʒɑ:məz] pl. – 147 **morbid** unhealthy – 152 **mother raper** (AE slang) a base, despicable person

A) Understanding the Text

1. What exactly is the task of the two detectives? How do they characterize their jobs themselves?
2. What are the feelings of Jones and Johnson towards white men on the one hand and blacks on the other?
3. How do people in Harlem react to the murder? Can you describe their behavior?

B) Interpretation and Discussion

1. Both detectives act and talk pretty cool. Think about the reasons why? What is the reason for their fatalistic behavior?
2. Do you think their attitude towards white people coming to Harlem is legitimate? What does the text say about the relationship between black and white people?
3. How could one explain the way in which people react to the murder?
4. The text portrays the situation in the slums of big cities. Think about why people live in such areas and why they don't move out.

C) Language Work

1. a) How does a *sedan* [siˈdæn] differ from a *coupé* [ˈku:pei, kuˈpei]? What other types of car do you know?
   b) The *accelerator* is one of three pedals in a non-automatic car. What are the other two? Name as many parts of a car as you can.
   c) Find German words for 'automobile' that are on the same stylistic level as 'tin lizzie' and 'struggle buggie'.
2. Describe the condition in which a *dilapidated* car would be.
3. *Arbiter, judge, referee* can all be translated as "Schiedsrichter". How do they differ in meaning?
4. The author describes his protagonists as 'cool'. Find other adjectives to describe their attitude and behavior.
5. *Joint* has various meanings. Find as many as you can, and decide which one is the correct one in line 33.
6. The text deals with crime, and there are many kinds of criminal offences mentioned by the author. Make a list of them and explain them in your own words. Can you think of any other offences not mentioned in the text?

7. Starting from your answer to Question 1c, discuss the relation between English *slang* and German *Umgangssprache, Gassensprache, Rotwelsch* etc. Consider such problems as: Who uses slang? Is it 'bad language'? Are some situations more suitable for the use of slang than others? Should German students learn English slang words?

D) Creative Writing

1. Write a scene from a detective novel, describing the arrest of a drug pusher (a shoot-out between a detective and a mafia killer; the interrogation of a mugger). Try to make use of the kind of language and style you have found in the above text.
2. Re-tell a German fairy tale, e.g. Der Wolf und die sieben Geißlein, in the manner of a 'tough' detective story.

2. The Reality Behind Words

by Jerzy Kosinski

One does not have to be a poet or a novelist – or an advertising sloganeer – to realize that words, like commanding officers and their men, can massacre innocent bystanders; and that often it is language that evokes in us a passion to embrace or reject others, to love or kill, to be free or be confined.

The case before the court: a multiple automobile crash on your friendly neighborhood highway, which has caused a few deaths, one or two dismemberments, and considerable property damage. All the defendants plead not guilty; they claim that just before the crash each of them was carefully driving his own friendly, properly registered, insured and recently inspected American-made motor vehicle. Their car models are called – as they are in actuality – Demon, Super Bee, Firebird, Tempest, Charger, Toronado, Centurion, Cutlass and Road Runner. The motor vehicles they inadvertently crashed into are named Thunderbird, Rebel, Cyclone, Swinger, Sting Ray, Dart, Barracuda and Fury. The accidents took place on a friendly community road called the expressway.

"... and therefore, Your Honor, when I saw this man trying to pass by me on the right in his Challenger, sure I stepped on it. Why, my Boss, which I just bought ..." protests one defendant.

"Objection, Your Honor. The car's name is irrelevant!" interrupts the prosecutor.

Should an objection against a name – a word – be sustained in this instance? Who but friendly defendants in most cases kill over fifty thousand friendly Americans yearly in car accidents on our friendly highways? Considering the pain, destruction and death these drivers caused, would it have been more appropriate if their four-wheel modes of transportation were named by car makers from Detroit – as indeed they ought to be – Collider, Veerer and Catapulter (for the young crowd, of course); Relapser (for those who think young); Maimer (medium-priced range); Polluter (top of the line); Autopsy-Coupe 400 (limited edition); Annihilator, Waster and Evacuator (the last three models available to military personnel at no extra cost with protective camouflage paint); and the compact Off-Roader?

Would a man driving the economical Super-Wound Convertible, for instance, race a lady smiling from her ash-colored Vista-Paralyso? Would a citizen in a supercharged Cougar dragrace against a couple of teenagers in their Wildcat, if instead he were driving a Custom-Disintegrator and they drove their parents' Hardhat-Vapido? Of course not!

From: Arthur Daigon, ed., *Violence, USA,* New York, 1975

Annotations

5 **to evoke** to call up – 6 **to be confined** to be kept shut up – 8 **dismemberment** G. Zerstückelung, Verstümmelung – 9 **property damage** G. Sachschaden – 9 **defendant** G. Angeklagter – 19 **to step on it** to increase speed of car – 21 **prosecutor** G. Staatsanwalt – 23 **to sustain an objection** G. (jur.) einem Einspruch stattgeben – 28 **to veer** to change direction – 29 **to relapse** to fall back again (e.g. into old habits) – 30 **to maim** G. verstümmeln – 30 **to pollute** to make dirty (environment) – 31 **to annihilate** [ə'naiəleit] to destroy completely – 33 **camouflage** ['kæməflɑːʒ] G. Tarnung – 34 **convertible** G. Kabriolett – 36 **supercharged** G. mit Kompressormotor – 36 **to dragrace** to make a race between two cars to find out which can speed up the faster – 37 **custom** (adj.) made according to personal order – 37 **to disintegrate** to break up into small pieces – 38 **hardhat** (sl.) conservative – 38 **vapid** dull, stupid

A) Understanding the Text

1. What kind of effects does Kosinski attribute to words?
2. According to Kosinski, who is responsible for
the accident – the friendly motor vehicle?
the friendly community road?
the drivers?
the names of the cars?
the producers of the cars?
3. What is the difference between the names of the cars involved in the imaginary accident and the car names suggested by Kosinski?
4. In the last paragraph, Kosinski presents a solution that is supposed to help avoid accidents. Describe his proposal.

B) Interpretation and Discussion

1. Why does Kosinski enumerate the names of all the cars involved in the accident?

2. What do you think of Kosinski's suggestion in the last passage?
3. What is Kosinski's reason for changing the actual car names into names like Collider, Maimer, etc.?
4. In his article, Kosinski uses the word "friendly" so often that it must have a special meaning. Discuss his intentions.
5. Compare German and American advertisements for automobiles. Describe and analyze the differences and similarities.

C) Language Work

1. Kosinski suggests such names as Collider, Polluter and Waster to bring out the real qualities of cars. How suitable would the following substitutes be: Rhino, Dolphin, Grizzly, Gazelle, Boomer, Bullet, Relaxer?
2. From American or British magazine and newspaper advertisements, compile a list of names whose appeal you think you can explain. For example, what appeal lies in "Tabu" as the name of a woman's perfume? In a man's scent called "007"? In a toothpaste called "Brisk"? A magazine called "Cosmopolitan"? A detergent called "Breeze"?

D) Creative Writing

Sometimes we conceal the true state of affairs by omitting certain unfavorable details and by using expressions which carry favorable overtones. For instance, if somebody wants to sell an old house which is in bad repair and lies a good distance from the nearest village, he might advertise it as "an historical cottage, quietly situated in scenic surroundings". Write two short passages about a hotel somewhere in Southern Europe, its amenities, surroundings, etc. One should be a text as a travel agent might write it to get people interested; the other text should be written from the point of view of a disappointed tourist. Make sure that both texts are about the same hotel and that only the attitude toward that hotel changes.

3. A Newspoem

Linda failed to return home
from a dance Friday night.
On Saturday
she admitted she had spent the night
with an Air Force lieutenant.

The Pratts decided on a punishment
that would "wake Linda up."
They ordered her
to shoot the dog
she had owned about two years.

On Sunday,
the Pratts and
Linda
took the dog into the desert
near their home.
They
had the girl
dig a shallow grave.
Then
Mrs. Pratt
grasped the dog between her hands and
Mr. Pratt
gave his daughter
a .22 caliber pistol
and told her
to shoot the dog.

Instead,
the girl
put the pistol
to her right temple
and shot herself.

The police said,
there were no charges
that could be filed
against the parents
except possibly
cruelty
to
animals.

From: *The New York Times,* February 7, 1968

Annotations

31 **temple** flat part of either side of the forehead (G. Schläfe) – 34 **to file a charge against s.o.** G. gegen jemanden Anklage erheben

A) Understanding the Text

1. Why did the Pratts want to punish Linda?
2. What sort of punishment did they intend to give her?
3. Why did Linda kill herself?
4. What did the police say? Paraphrase the last paragraph.

B) Interpretation and Discussion

1. Do you think Linda's behavior justifies any punishment at all?
2. Can you imagine what the Pratts had in mind when they decided on this kind of punishment?
3. Who is guilty of what happened in this tragic incident –
   - Linda who slept with the lieutenant?
   - Mr. and Mrs. Pratt who ordered the dog shot?
   - the lieutenant who seduced Linda?
   - the police who could not file any charges against the parents?
   - the society which permitted this to happen and did not interfere with it?
4. Do you find it unjust that no legal steps can be taken in this case?

4. Watts-Miami: it's a scary analogy

by George Mair

It was like seeing the same tragic movie over again and it left the same sick feeling in my gut. The videotape and film I saw of the recent Miami riots was, for me, like reliving the Watts riots of 1965 that I covered in person. There were the same black rage; the same cries of frustration; the same hatred of the white-dominated system, and the same mindless violence visited mostly against one's own kind.

The reasons for Miami 1980 are essentially the same as the reasons for Watts 1965: a white-controlled society that denies decent schools, housing and employment and that keeps the blacks under control through insensitive police power.

The Watts riot was triggered by the traffic arrest of a black man named Donald Frye on a hot night in August 1965. The Miami riot was triggered by the acquittal of four white cops (one of Cuban descent) who had arrested Arthur McDuffie for speeding and were charged with beating him to death. The Miami situation was made worse by the influx of Cuban and Haitian refugees because the Cubans are given special privileges and immediate help by Washington. By contrast, the black Haitian refugees have been jerked around by Washington, treated differently from other refugees and denied help of any kind.

During the Watts riot, almost all the white politicians stayed away from the area and the explosive situation. They let the cops and the National Guard do the dirty work. That's exactly what happened in Miami – most politicians or so-called leaders, black or white, did nothing.

If Miami follows the Watts analogy, the next step is to find out who the leaders of the black rioting were and get them on some government payroll at a fat salary. That co-opts them out of the community and renders them impotent to challenge the white-run system. Most of the black riot leaders of the 1960s are now in big government positions and part of the problem instead of being part of the solution.

Oh, the Watts-Miami analogy may not hold up on every count, but it is close enough to be scary.

Los Angeles Times Syndicate

Annotations

1 **Watts** district in Los Angeles where race riots took place in 1965 – 1 **Miami** [mai'æmi] – 1 **scary** causing fear – 4 **gut** stomach – 5 **to cover** (in journalism) to report – 8 **to visit (anger) on** (rarely **against**) to direct against – 11 **insensitive** G. rücksichtslos – 14 **to trigger (off)** to start – 15 **acquittal** G. Freispruch – 15 **cop** (coll.) policeman – 16 **to speed** to drive too fast – 16 **to charge with** to accuse of – 17 **influx** arrival – 20 **to jerk around** to treat roughly and unfairly – 27 **to get s.o. on the payroll** to employ – 28 **to co-opt** to make s.o. a member of one's own group – 29 **impotent** unable – 29 **to challenge** to question the rightness of – 29 **white-run** controlled by whites – 32 **to hold up** to be valid – 32 **on every count** G. in allen Punkten

A) Understanding the Text

1. What were the reasons for the Miami riots?
2. What did the politicians do in order to curb the riots?
3. How can the establishment "co-opt" the leaders of riots?

B) Interpretation and Discussion

1. Discuss the author's idea of "insensitive police power". How can "police power" be "insensitive" when confronting a howling mob, bent on destruction, looting and blood-letting?
2. The author has a very low opinion of black leaders who subsequent to riots went on "some government payroll at a fat salary". Will promotion to governmental agencies automatically corrupt the leaders of a social or political movement?

C) Language Work

1. Replace the word in italics with another word or phrase of similar meaning.

   I had been present in Watts fifteen years ago, and watching the film of the *recent* Miami riots was like seeing the same *tragic* movie over again. There was the same black *rage,* the same *mindless* violence. The reason for both *riots* is *essentially* the same: a white-dominated society that *denies* the blacks a decent life.

2. The endings *-er, -or, -ar* (all pronounced /ə/) and *-ist, -an, -ian* are used for a *person who does* or *is connected with something.* Add the correct suffix to these words, making slight changes in the spelling where it is necessary (e.g. Italy – Italian):

politics	economics	Paris	motor
law	school	New York	lie
govern	employ	Luther	

5. The ghetto blight remains

by David E. Rosebaum, New York Times

On the surface, there has been enormous progress since the urban riots of the late 1960s. It is a salt-and-pepper workforce now that pours out at lunch-time from the steel, glass and concrete skyscrapers that have come to dominate downtown America.

There is hardly an office without black professionals, hardly a community without a black man or woman anchoring the television news, hardly a city without a once poor neighborhood being renovated by the well-to-do.

Inside the ghettos, however, the blight remains. For the majority of Americans who normally pay little attention to the big-city slums, the trouble in Miami was a reminder of how little some things have really changed. Consider the following:

● **INCOME.** In 1969, the median family income in central cities was 83 percent of the income of people living in the suburbs. By 1977, according to a Census Bureau study released in May, it had fallen to 79 percent.

During that period, the income of suburban families kept pace with inflation, while that of families in the cities did not. Furthermore, the proportion of black families with incomes below the poverty line remained steady at between 25 and 30 percent.

"It would be incorrect to say there was no improvement in the economic status of blacks," said Bernard E. Anderson, an economist who is director for social sciences at the Rockefeller Foundation.

"Some persons achieved notable progress and moved closer to the enjoyment of economic security. Such persons, however, represented the minority of blacks; for the community as a whole, the decade, at best, was a standoff."

● **JOBS.** Throughout the 1970s, in boom times and busts, the unemployment rate among blacks was twice that of whites, and never lower than 8 percent. The unemployment rate of black teen-agers was well over 30 percent throughout the decade. More and more factories moved out of the cities each year, and manufacturing jobs, historically the first step into the job market for the urban poor, have dried up.

● **EDUCATION.** The most encouraging signs of progress are in the area of education. The proportion of black high school dropouts declined in the last decade from 33 percent to 25 percent, and the proportion of black high school graduates going to college increased from 35 percent to 42 percent. Today, black high school graduates are as likely as whites to go to college.

Those figures, however, may be somewhat misleading because they leave aside the question of quality.

Inner-city schools have increasingly become institutions for the poor, and, in the words of Bernard C. Watson, an education specialist at Temple University, "the education too many children receive in these classrooms is an absolute disgrace."

As for higher education, 42 percent of black students are in two-year community colleges, as against 33 percent of white students, and half of the blacks in college attend schools with historically all-black enrollments.

● **HEALTH.** The life expectancy of blacks remains well below that of whites. In recent years, the infant and maternal mortality rates for blacks has improved but not so fast as the white rates have improved. On the average, blacks spend half of what whites spend for health care, and medicaid payments to whites are much higher than to blacks, primarily because blacks are still discriminated against in admission to nursing homes.

● **HOUSING.** In the cities, the percentage of blacks owning their homes increased slightly from 33 percent to 37 percent during the 1970s, but studies show that blacks are less likely than whites to have such amenities as air conditioning and more than one complete bath, and more likely to lack some plumbing and kitchen facilities and central heating. In many cities, rehabilitation and new construction have not kept up with population increases.

Looking at such statistics, Vernon E. Jordan Jr., director of the National Urban League, concluded recently that "the '70s were not a time of progress within black America."

Moreover, Jordan said, "statistics alone do not tell the full story, for there were also signs of further alienation from the majority as black people sought jobs that were not there, black children left the public schools without the tools that would enable them to compete with others, government grew cold and indifferent and hope for a better day grew fainter and fainter in the hearts of many."

Not all experts in urban affairs are pessimistic. Richard P. Nathan, director of the Urban and Regional Research Program at Princeton University, said he believed that 1980 census figures might show the revitalization of at least some cities.

But everyone in the field agrees that blacks in general and those in the cities in particular will be the people hardest hit by the current recession. In Detroit, the city that so far has suffered most from the economic slowdown, the unemployment rate in some black neighborhoods is put at 35 percent or more.

The dominant political view nowadays was expressed by Sen. Pete V. Domenici, R-N.M., during the House-Senate conference debate on the federal budget.

Another conferee asserted that the disturbance in Miami was evidence of the need for increased government social programs. "The problem in Florida," Domenici responded, "indicated not that we need more funding for programs but that, with the billions and billions we have spent on social programs, we still have a Florida."

Annotations

1 **blight** condition of disorder and ugliness – 4 **salt-and-pepper** white and black – 4 **work force** workers considered as a body – 5 **concrete** G. Beton – 6 **downtown** business center of an American town or city – 8 **to anchor** G. moderieren – 14 **median** average – 16 **Census Bureau** G. Statistisches Bundesamt – 27 **stand-off** (sports) G. Unentschieden – 28 **bust** period of reduced business activity and high unemployment – 35 **dropout** person who stops attending school without completing the course – 45 **community college** G. Hochschule mit teils akadem., teils techn. und berufsvorbereitenden Ausbildungsgängen – 47 **enrollment** number of people attending – 49 **maternal** of a mother – 51 **medicaid** government program providing medical aid, esp. for old and poor persons – 53 **nursing home** G. Pflegeheim – 56 **amenity** [əˈmeniti] (often pl.) G. Komfort – 58 **plumbing facilities** G. sanitäre Einrichtungen – 58 **rehabilitation** (of houses) putting back into good condition – 64 **alienation** [ˌeiljəˈneiʃn] G. Entfremdung – 71 **to revitalize** to put new strength or power into – 78 **Sen.** Senator – 79 **R** Republican – 79 **NM** New Mexico – 81 **conferee** member of a conference – 83 **to fund** to provide money

The disparities behind Miami's troubles

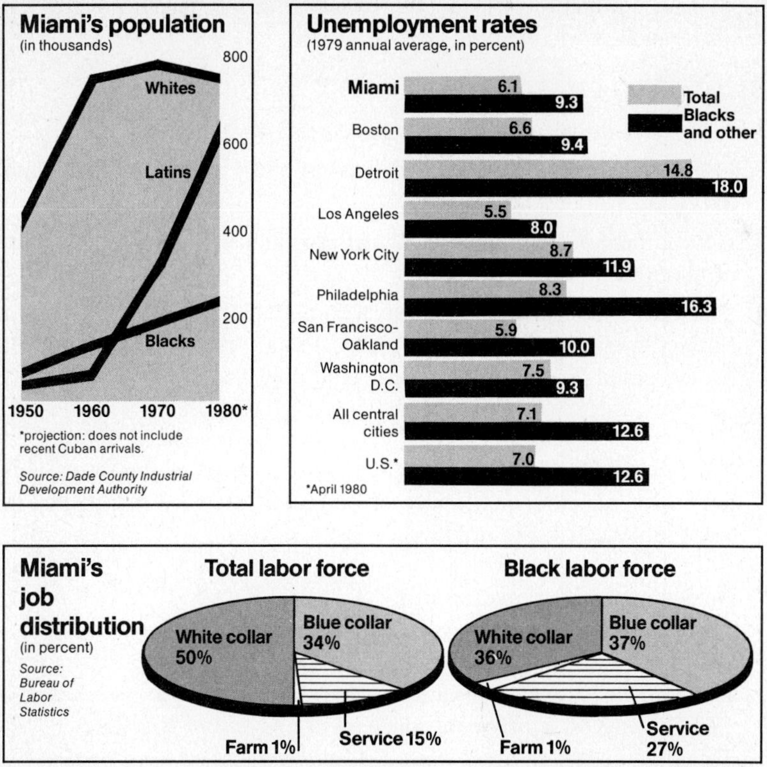

(nach einer Veröffentlichung der New York Times)

A) Understanding the Text

1. Describe the surface changes mentioned by D. E. Rosebaum.
2. How has the average family income developed in the city centers (where many blacks live) and in the suburbs (where there is a white majority)?
3. Paraphrase B. E. Anderson's statement on the economic status of blacks in your own words.
4. Why will young blacks find less jobs in the cities?
5. Progress in the area of education is called "a most encouraging sign" by Rosebaum. But, then, what do other education specialists say concerning the quality of a black youth's education?
6. What is said about health? What are the reasons for the differences between health conditions of blacks and whites?
7. Describe the housing situation of blacks.

8. Compare the views of V. E. Jordan Jr. and those of R. P. Nathan.
9. Explain the nature of inequality indicated in the diagram of the job distribution in Miami.

B) Interpretation and Discussion

1. What does the idea of "economic security" mean to you?
2. Is there a similarity between the situation of the American blacks and the "guest workers" in Germany?
3. Do you believe that increased social programs can cure the situation of minorities?
4. The author maintains that "statistics do not tell the full story". Do you agree with this negative view of empirical data? What other factors must be accounted for in order to understand the situation of minorities?

C) Language Work

1. The infinitive can often be used in place of a clause, particularly if this has future meaning or the idea of obligation. Replace the clauses in these sentences by an infinitive.

   He is a man *whom you can trust.*
   There is no one there *who can help me.*
   Let's hurry, there's a lot *which must be done.*
   Don't forget that you have a train *which you must catch.*
   Can you suggest somewhere *where we can go for our holidays?*
   This is an occassion *which must not be forgotten.*

2. Place the adverbs supplied in the correct place in the sentence.
   She was born. (in 1964, in Dallas)
   They returned. (with their friends, at eleven o'clock, to their hotel)
   He went to fetch his coat. (upstairs, a few minutes ago)
   The goalkeeper leaned. (all through the game, lazily, against his goal)
   Take the third door. (upstairs, on the left, in the passage)
   He spoke to the crowd. (clearly, with deliberation)

III. Fear and Anonymity in Everyday Life

In the 60's and 70's, Americans have been forced to absorb more changes than probably any other generation in American history. The most important of these changes may have been the virtual breakdown of a sense of "belonging" and the subsequent rise of feelings of isolation and alienation. Anonymous institutions, Americans have come to feel, are gaining more and more control over their lives. The American who was taught to be proud of his self-reliant frontier ancestors finds himself confronted with "the corporate state", its functionaries, and soulless bureaucracy. His life has become increasingly regulated, and more often than not, he finds the meaning of his life reduced to the functions he can fulfill for "the system". The question of a meaningful identity in private as well as in public life has become paramount. Tensions and unrest in the over-all social structure foster a withdrawal from contemporary reality as effectively as the machinelike indifference of the system itself.

Annotations

4 **virtual** [ˈvəːtʃuəl] G. faktisch – 5 **subsequent** later, following – 5 **alienation** critical detachment from (G. Entfremdung) – 9 **corporate state** G. Staat als Machtapparat, als festgefügtes System – 13 **paramount** most important – 13 **tension** G. (psych.) Spannung – 14 **foster** to care for, to help the growth of

1. The Good Things

We hear a lot about war, or hurricanes that hit our shore
We hear a lot about hard times and a good deal more about the crimes.
That make the front pages of our news.
But, all that does is sing the blues...
About America!

Now what of the good things in our lives?
About the men who love their wives?
Who take their kids when they go fishin',
And spend their workin' days just wishin'
To make things better!

A fireman who climbs a tree and sets a little kitten free
A policeman who helps you cross the avenue.
A man who stops when you're broken down
And asks if you need a lift to town,
Or simply says, "Friend, what can I do?"

Have you stopped at a grocery store and watched a kid who's bit off more
Than his five or ten-cent piece can chew?
He needs just two cents or three, to get that soda-pop you see!
And you get that feelin'... "Why not?" And you come through.

And how about on a Sunday morning, the sun's up high, the day is borning.
And church bells break the stillness in the sky?
And all your neighbors and your friends climb in the family car again
And go to church, and never question, "Why?"

Then you look at the U.S.A., the folks at work, their kids at play,
And lookin' back you see how hard they've tried
To keep this country free and strong.
And somehow, you've known all along,
The answer's here! Right in your own back yard!

For as long as you believe in love... in faith... hope... and God above,
The future of this land of ours is strong.
And most of us feel just that way, and that's the truth! So let us say,
"America... can't be so very wrong."

From: John Wayne, *"America, Why I Love Her"*, Music by Billy Liebert, Words by John Mitchum and Howard Barnes, (Copyright RCA Records, New York, 1973)

Annotations

19 **soda pop** lemonade – 20 **to come through** to do what is needed – 21 **borning** (dial.) being born

A) Understanding the Text

1. Sum up the negative things that, in Wayne's words, "make the front page" of America's news.
2. Compile a list of "the good things" which John Wayne mentions.
3. What does the poem present as a basic condition for a strong and happy future of America?

B) Interpretation and Discussion

1. What is meant by the phrase "that make the front page of our news"?
2. What is John Wayne's basic opinion of today's America? In how far does it differ from the bad news indicated in the first stanza?
3. What does Wayne mean by the phrase "The answer's here! Right in your own back yard!"?
4. Compare the attitudes of John Wayne and Jack Anderson towards the present state of their country. Are there differences, similarities, contradictions?

Heller, Something Happened

Joseph Heller is the author of the biggest-selling "serious novel" in American publishing history. His first book, *Catch-22,* sold more than 10,000,000 copies. Thirteen years later, in 1974, Heller published *Something Happened,* his second book, and it became an immediate international bestseller. It is a stream-of-neurosis peek into the head of your "average American": family man, corporate man, and psychotic monster. Bob Slocum lives in a nice house in Connecticut with a wife, a daughter and two sons and works as a middle-management executive in communications. He is exhausted by the routine of everyday life, petrified with boredom, drained of any capacity for joyfulness, and, worst of all, he is scared out of his wits by the very routine and material success of his life, afraid that "something will happen". Heller's description of Slocum's "normal hell" is a truly disquieting picture of the middle-class experience in a golden cage from which there is no escape and whose dominant features are faceless dread and joyless well-being.

Annotations

6 **stream-of-neurosis** cf. stream-of-consciousness: in literature, the expression of a person's (neurotic) thoughts as they flow in his mind – 6 **to peek** to look quickly – 10 **to petrify** to turn into stone

2. Somehow the Time Passes

The company is benevolent. The people, for the most part, are nice, and the atmosphere, for the most part, is convivial. The decor of the offices, particularly in the reception rooms and anterooms, is bright and colorful. There is lots of orange and lots of sea green. There are lots of office parties. We get all legal holidays off and take days off with pay whenever we need them. We have many three- and four-day weekends....

Every two weeks we are paid with machine-processed checks manufactured out of stiff paper (they are not thick enough to be called cardboard) that are patterned precisely with neat, rectangular holes and words of formal, official warning in small, black, block letters that the checks must not be spindled, torn, defaced, stapled, or mutilated in any other way. (They must only be cashed.) If not for these words, it would never occur to me to do anything else with my check but deposit it.... What would happen if, deliberately, calmly, with malice aforethought and obvious premeditation, I disobeyed? I know what would happen: nothing. Nothing would happen. And the knowledge depresses me. Some girl downstairs I never saw before (probably with a bad skin also) would simply touch a few keys on some kind of steel key punch that would set things right again, and it would be as though I had not disobeyed at all. My act of rebellion would be absorbed like rain on an ocean and leave no trace. I would not cause a ripple.

I suppose it is just about impossible for someone like me to rebel anymore and produce any kind of lasting effect....

We have twenty-nine offices now, twelve in this country, two in Canada, four in Latin America, and eleven overseas. We used to have one in Cuba, but that was lost. We average three suicides a year: two men, usually on the middle-executive level, kill themselves every twelve months, almost always by gunshot, and one girl, usually unmarried, separated, or divorced, who generally does the job with sleeping pills. Salaries are high, vacations are long....

Most of us like working here, even though we are afraid, and do not long to leave for jobs with other companies. We make money and have fun. We read books and go to plays. And somehow the time passes.

Green now thinks I am conspiring to undermine him. He is wrong. For one thing, I don't have the initiative; for another, I don't have the nerve; and for still another thing, I guess I really like and admire Green in many respects (even though I also hate and resent him in many others), and I know I am probably safer working for him than I would be working for anyone else–even for Andy Kagle in the Sales Department if they did decide to move me and my department from Green's department to Kagle's department.

In many ways and on many occasions Green and I are friends and allies and do helpful, sometimes considerate things for each other. Often, I protect and defend him when he is late or forgetful with work of his own, and I frequently give him credit for good work from my department that he does not deserve. But I never tell him I do this; and I never let him know when I hear anything favorable about him. I enjoy seeing Green apprehensive. I'm pleased he distrusts me (it does wonders for my self-esteem), and I do no more than necessary to reassure him.

And I am the best friend he has here.

So I scare Green, and Green scares White, and White scares Black, and Black scares Brown and Green, and Brown scares me and Green and Andy Kagle, and all of this is absolutely true, because Horace White really is afraid of conversation with Jack Green, and Johnny Brown, who bulldozes everyone around him with his strong shoulders, practical mind, and tough, outspoken mouth, is afraid of Lester Black, who protects him.

I know it's true, because I worked this whole color wheel out one dull, wet afternoon on one of those organizational charts I am always constructing when I grow bored with my work.

I am bored with my work very often now. Everything routine that comes in I pass along to somebody else. This makes my boredom worse. It's a real problem to decide whether it's more boring to do something boring than to pass along everything boring that comes in to somebody else and then have nothing to do at all.

Actually, I enjoy my work when the assignments are large and urgent and somewhat frightening and will come to the attention of many people. I get scared, and am unable to sleep at night, but I usually perform at my best under this stimulating kind of pressure and enjoy my job the most. I handle all of these important projects myself, and I rejoice with tremendous pride and vanity in the compliments I receive when I do them well (as I always do). But between such peaks of challenge and elation there is monotony and despair. (And I find, too, that once I've succeeded in impressing somebody, I'm not much excited about impressing that same person again; there is a large, emotional letdown after I survive each crisis, a kind of empty, tragic disappointment, and last year's threat, opportunity, and inspiration are often this year's inescapable tedium. I frequently feel I'm being taken advantage of merely because I'm asked to do the work I'm paid to do.)

From: Joseph Heller, *Something Happened,* London, Jonathan Cape, 1974

Annotations

2 **benevolent** [-ˈ---] kind and helpful – 3 **convivial** merry – 3 **décor** [deiˈkɔː] furnishing – 4 **anteroom** [ˈænti-] G. Vorzimmer – 8 **machine-processed** printed by computer – 10 **rectangular** G. rechteckig – 11 **to spindle** G. aufspießen – 12 **to deface** to spoil the appearance of (by writing on etc.) – 12 **to staple** G. mit Heftklammern versehen – 12 **to mutilate** to destroy the use of – 14 **to deposit** [diˈpɔzit] to place in a bank – 15 **with malice aforethought and obvious premeditation** (jur.) G. vorsätzlich – 18 **key** G. Taste – 19 **key punch** G. Lochkartenmaschine – 21 **ripple** very small wave – 26 **suicide** [ˈsjuisaid] G. Selbstmord – 27 **executive** [igˈzekjutiv] G. (leitender) Angestellter – 28 **divorced** G. geschieden – 29 **vacation** period of holiday – 34 **to conspire** to make secret plans – 37 **to resent** [riˈzent] to feel angry at – 42 **ally** person who gives help or support – 45 **to give s.o. credit for** to give praise or approval – 47 **apprehensive** uneasy, worried – 54 **to bulldoze** G. einschüchtern – 58 **organizational chart** G. graphische Übersicht einer Organisation – 65 **assignment** task – 71 **elation** high spirits – 74 **letdown** disappointment – 76 **tedium** [ˈtiːdjəm] boredom

A) Understanding the Text

1. What are the protagonist's working conditions?
2. How does he rate his chances to change any of the given regulations controlling his working days?
3. What does he say about the company's employees?
4. What does Green think of the first person narrator (whose name is Bob Slocum)?
5. How does Slocum feel towards Green, his superior?
6. Describe the relationship between Green and Slocum.

7. What is the determining force in the relationship between the employees of the company?
8. Try to determine Slocum's attitude towards his job.
   Take into consideration what he says about boredom, pressure, and vanity.

B) Interpretation and Discussion

1. What do you think of – what he calls – "the company's benevolence"?
2. What do the protagonist's meditations on the checks indicate? What is the role of an individual in such a company? What would or could be changed by an individual's act of rebellion?
3. How can you reconcile his positive description of working conditions with the "average" suicide rate?
4. What, do you think, are the motivating forces behind people's behavior – innate qualities or certain social circumstances?
5. Compare the situation in this company with that in companies you know. Compare it with the board of teachers at your school, or with social relations in your own course. Are there parallels?
6. Can you give an interpretation of Bob Slocum's psychological condition?
7. Do you think that Heller paints a realistic picture of working conditions in a modern office? If possible, consider your own experiences of office work or those of friends or relatives.

C) Language Work

1. Underline the following adverbs in the text and comment on their position in the sentence: really, probably, often, frequently, never, always, usually
2. Put the adverbs given in brackets in suitable places in the sentences

   Mrs. Mogg is not Annie's aunt. (really)
   This mountain has been climbed before. (probably, never)
   She sat brooding. (often, there)
   I've had the 'flu. (fortunately, never)
   He walks. (round the park, usually, before supper, twice)
3. Put in the correct prepositions where necessary (in, on, about, to, with, of, at):

   I usually enjoy … reading, but … this book I got bored very quickly.

   It has come … my attention, Mr. Orton, that you resent … your job in the Sales Department and that you have developed a habit … passing work … … somebody else.

Janet is quite excited ... the fact that she has finally succeeded ... finding an apartment.

I often work ... night, and I am ... my best after midnight.

D) Creative Writing

Write an essay on the role of fear and anxiety in your everyday school-life.

"Mr. Kendall then said, 'I withdraw that last remark.' Mr. Brook then withdrew his last remark. Mr. Cole then withdrew his remark. Mr. Kohler, his. Mr. O'Toole, his. Mr. Swanson, his . . ."

Drawing by Dana Fradon;

Interpretation and Discussion

Describe the situation presented in this cartoon. Where is its satirical point?

Paul Simon (born 1942): graduate of Brooklyn Law School, had a number of top hits in the years between 1967 and 1970 as one part of the pop music duo Simon and Garfunkel. Since 1970 he has been writing and singing on his own with considerable and continuous success. His songs have always reflected interpersonal relationships, the conditions of life in industrial mass society, and the situation of drop-outs, outsiders, and determined individualists.

3. Sounds of Silence

by Paul Simon (1964)

Hello darkness, my old friend,
I've come to talk with you again,
Because a vision softly creeping
Left its seeds while I was sleeping;
And the vision that was planted in my brain
Still remains within the Sounds of Silence.

In restless dreams I walked alone
Narrow streets of cobblestone.
'Neath the halo of a streetlamp,
I turned my collar to the cold and damp
When my eyes were stabbed
By the flash of a neon light,
That split the night and touched the Sound of Silence.

And in the naked light I saw
Ten thousand people, maybe more.
People talking without speaking,
People hearing without listening,
People writing songs that voices never share
And no one dare disturb the Sound of Silence.

"Fools!" said I, "You do not know
Silence like a cancer grows.
Hear my words that I might teach you,
Take my arms that I might reach you."
But my words like silent raindrops fell,
And echoed in the wells of silence.

And the people bowed and prayed
To the neon God they made.
And the sign flashed out its warning
In the words that it was forming,
And the sign said, "The words of the prophets
Are written on subway walls and tenement halls."
And whispered in the Sound of Silence.

Annotations

5 **vision** ['viʒən] G. Vision – 10 **cobblestone** rounded stone used for paving, G. Kopfstein – 11 **halo** ['heiləu] (here:) circle of light round a lamp – 23 **cancer** ['kænsə] G. Krebs(geschwür) – 33 **tenement hall** G. Flur eines (ärmlichen) Mietshauses

A) Understanding the Text

1. Describe the "vision that was planted in (the singer's) brain".
2. What does the singer say about the God that people made?
3. What does he see in the naked neon light?
4. The fourth stanza consists mainly of direct speech. Who speaks there? Is it a dream or reality?

B) Interpretation and Discussion

1. There are many metaphors in the text. Discuss the meaning of
   - sounds of silence
   - silence like a cancer grows
   - the words echoed in the wells of silence
   - neon God
   - The words of the prophets are written on subway walls and tenement halls
2. What does the author mean by "people talking without speaking, people hearing without listening"?
3. Who does the singer talk to? Whom does he call an "old friend?" What does that mean?
4. Try to summarize in a few words the topic of this song. Is it a song on the future of mankind, the materialistic attitudes of people, or what?

C) Creative Writing

1. When Paul Simon says "my words like silent raindrops fell" he is adding emphasis, by means of this comparison, to the basic idea that his words

went unnoticed. Find similarly vivid comparisons to give force to experiences and ideas of your own. Try the following to start with:

She smiled happily. Her smile was like... Her face was ... when she smiled; Her mouth...

I was very disappointed. The discovery that ... hit me like ...; I was so ... by my disappointment ...

2. Using a tune that you know, write a little song of your own about feeling lonely in a crowd; looking at faces in a public place; watching a bird flying high up in the sky; or any topic of your choice.

4. 38 Who Saw Murder Didn't Call the Police

by Martin Gansberg

For more than half an hour 38 respectable, law-abiding citizens in Queens watched a killer stalk and stab a woman in three separate attacks in Kew Gardens.

Twice their chatter and the sudden glow of their bedroom lights interrupted him and frightened him off. Each time he returned, sought her out, and stabbed her again. Not one person telephoned the police during the assault; one witness called after the woman was dead.

That was two weeks ago today.

Still shocked is Assistant Chief Inspector Frederick M. Lussen, in charge of the borough's detectives and a veteran of 25 years of homicide investigations. He can give a matter-of-fact recitation on many murders. But the Kew Gardens slaying baffles him - not because it is a murder, but because the "good people" failed to call the police.

"As we have reconstructed the crime," he said, "the assailant had three chances to kill this woman during a 35-minute period. He returned twice to complete the job. If we had been called when he first attacked, the woman might not be dead now."

This is what the police say happened beginning at 3:20 a. m. in the staid, middle-class, tree-lined Austin Street area:

Twenty-eight-year-old Catherine Genovese, who was called Kitty by almost everyone in the neighborhood, was returning home from her job as manager of a bar in Hollis. She parked her red Fiat in a lot adjacent to the Kew Gardens Long Island Rail Road Station, facing Mowbray Place. Like many residents of the neighborhood, she had parked there day after day since her arrival from Connecticut a year ago, although the railroad frowns on the practice.

She turned off the lights of her car, locked the door, and started to walk the 100 feet to the entrance of her apartment at 82-70 Austin Street, which is in a

Tudor building, with stores on the first floor and apartments on the second. The entrance to the apartment is in the rear of the building because the front is rented to retail stores. At night the quiet neighborhood is shrouded in the slumbering darkness that marks most residential areas.

Miss Genovese noticed a man at the far end of the lot, near a seven-story apartment house at 82-40 Austin Street. She halted. Then, nervously, she headed up Austin Street toward Lefferts Boulevard, where there is a call box to the 102nd Police Precinct in nearby Richmond Hill.

She got as far as a street light in front of a bookstore before the man grabbed her. She screamed. Lights went on in the 10-story apartment house at 82-67 Austin Street, which faces the bookstore. Windows slid open and voices punctuated the early-morning stillness.

Miss Genovese screamed: "Oh, my God, he stabbed me! Please help me! Please help me!"

From one of the upper windows in the apartment house, a man called down: "Let that girl alone!"

The assailant looked up at him, shrugged, and walked down Austin Street toward a white sedan parked a short distance away. Miss Genovese struggled to her feet.

Lights went out. The killer returned to Miss Genovese, now trying to make her way around the side of the building by the parking lot to get to her apartment. The assailant stabbed her again.

"I'm dying!" she shrieked. "I'm dying!"

Windows were opened again, and lights went on in many apartments. The assailant got into his car and drove away. Miss Genovese staggered to her feet. A city bus, O-10, the Lefferts Boulevard line to Kennedy International Airport, passed. It was 3:35 a. m.

The assailant returned. By then, Miss Genovese had crawled to the back of the building, where the freshly painted brown doors to the apartment house held out hope for safety. The killer tried the first door; she wasn't there. At the second door, 82-62 Austin Street, he saw her slumped on the floor at the foot of the stairs. He stabbed her a third time - fatally.

It was 3:50 by the time the police received their first call, from a man who was a neighbor of Miss Genovese. In two minutes they were at the scene. The neighbor, a 70-year-old woman, and another woman were the only persons on the street. Nobody else came forward.

The man explained that he had called the police after much deliberation. He had phoned a friend in Nassau County for advice and then he had crossed the roof of the building to the apartment of the elderly woman to get her to make the call.

"I didn't want to get involved," he sheepishly told the police.

Six days later, the police arrested Winston Moseley, a 29-year-old business-machine operator, and charged him with the homicide. Moseley had no previous record. He is married, has two children and owns a home at 133-19 Sutter Avenue, South Ozone Park, Queens. On Wednesday, a court committed him to Kings County Hospital for psychiatric observation.

When questioned by the police, Moseley also said that he had slain Mrs. Annie May Johnson, 24, of 146-12 133rd Avenue, Jamaica, on Feb. 29 and Barbara Kralik, 15, of 174-17 140th Avenue, Springfield Gardens, last July. In the Kralik case, the police are holding Alvin L. Mitchell, who is said to have confessed that slaying.

The police stressed how simple it would have been to have gotten in touch with them. "A phone call," said one of the detectives, "would have done it." The police may be reached by dialing "O" for operator or SPring 7-3100.

Today witnesses from the neighborhood, which is made up of one-family homes in the $35,000 to $60,000 range with the exception of the two apartment houses near the railroad station, find it difficult to explain why they didn't call the police.

A housewife, knowingly if quite casual, said, "We thought it was a lover's quarrel."A husband and wife both said, "Frankly, we were afraid." They seemed aware of the fact that events might have been different. A distraught woman, wiping her hands in her apron, said, "I didn't want my husband to get involved."

One couple, now willing to talk about that night, said they heard the first screams. The husband looked thoughtfully at the bookstore where the killer first grabbed Miss Genovese.

"We went to the window to see what was happening," he said, "but the light from our bedroom made it difficult to see the street." The wife, still apprehensive, added: "I put out the light and we were able to see better." Asked why they hadn't called the police, she shrugged and replied: "I don't know."

A man peeked out from a slight opening in the doorway to his apartment and rattled off an account of the killer's second attack. Why hadn't he called the police at the time? "I was tired," he said without emotion. "I went back to bed."

It was 4:25 a.m. when the ambulance arrived to take the body of Miss Genovese. It drove off. "Then," a solemn police detective said, "the people came out."

From: *The New York Times,* March 27, 1964

Annotations

3 **Queens** one of the five boroughs, or districts, of New York City – 3 **law-abiding** obeying the law – 4 **to stalk** to hunt (usu. an animal) by following quietly and staying

hidden - 4 **to stab** to wound with a knife - 7 **to seek s.o. out** G. aufspüren - 8 **assault** sudden violent attack - 11 **in charge of** responsible for - 12 **homicide** murder - 14 **slaying** (lit. or journalistic) murder, killing - 14 **to baffle** to puzzle - 16 **assailant** G. Angreifer - 20 **staid** quiet, conservative - 24 **lot** G. Grundstück - 24 **adjacent to** [ə'dʒeisənt] very close, next to - 27 **to frown on s.th.** to disapprove of - 31 **Tudor** (style) G. (neu)gotischer Baustil - 33 **retail store** G. Einzelhandelsgeschäft - 33 **to shroud** to cover and hide - 39 **to grab** to seize with a sudden rough movement - 42 **to punctuate** to interrupt - 48 **sedan** [si'dæn] G. Limousine - 61 **to slump** to collapse - 62 **fatal** ['feitl] causing death - 67 **deliberation** careful consideration - 71 **sheepish** G. schüchtern, verlegen - 73 **to charge s.o. with s.th.** to accuse of - 74 **record** G. (hier) Vorstrafen - 75 **to commit s.o.** (usu. pass.) G. (in psych. Anstalt) einweisen - 89 **casual** ['kæʒuəl] showing little sense of responsibility - 91 **distraught** very anxious and troubled - 99 **apprehensive** worried, anxious - 102 **to peek** to look quickly and secretly - 103 **to rattle off** to say s.th. in a fast careless way - 107 **solemn** ['sɔləm] serious, grave

A) Understanding the Text

1. Describe the sequence of events.
2. Does the Assistant Chief Inspector attest to the inevitability of Miss Genovese's death?
3. What are the residents' responses?
4. What are the residents' excuses for not having called the police?
5. What happened to the man who was charged with the homicide?

B) Interpretation and Discussion

1. No explicit judgments are made in the text. Discuss the author's choice of narrative strategies. Would a more emotional or dramatic account of the event be more effective?
2. Why did the murderer attack Miss Genovese? Discuss the probability of such an attack in a German city.
3. Do you understand why the neighbors acted the way they did? How would you react in a similar situation?
4. The author uses inverted commas to indicate a certain lack of qualities in "the good people". Discuss the fundamental qualities of a truly "good neighborhood".

C) Language Work

1. Here are some expressions that can serve to express contrast between two ideas:
   although, though, but, in spite of, despite, yet, however, all the same, still, even so
   Choose suitable expressions from this list, or use others of your own choice, to link the following sentences.

a) A woman was violently attacked three times. The neighbors merely watched.
b) She desperately cried for help. Nobody came to help her.
c) 38 respectable citizens had watched the drama. Only one witness called the police.
d) It would have been simple to phone the police. Nobody made the effort.
e) No doubt these people consider themselves respectable. Even a case of murder does not stir them.

2. Make up similar sentences of your own.
3. Make a list of words and expressions related to police work and legal action that are used in this text. Do you know any more words from these fields?
4. Supposing you were a police reporter, give a brief account of the crime, of the killer's arrest, and of the legal procedure to be expected. Use as many of the words that you listed under 3. as possible.

D) Creative Writing

Write a newspaper comment on this incident, expressing as forcefully as you can your indignation at these people's indifference, and analyzing possible causes of their attitude.

Allen Ginsberg (born 1926): With Jack Kerouac, Neal Cassidy, Carl Solomon and Gregory Corso he belonged to the so-called Beat Generation, a protest movement of the 1950's. In the 1960's he joined the hippie movement. He is well known for his poetry and prose books. His most famous works of poetry are "Howl", "Kaddish", and "Reality Sandwiches". His works deal with the search for a meaningful identity under the conditions of an extremely technologized society.

5. Allen Ginsberg, Moloch

What sphinx of cement and aluminum bashed open their skulls and ate up their brains and imagination?
Moloch! Solitude! Filth! Ugliness! Ashcans and unobtainable dollars! Children screaming under the stairways! Boys sobbing in armies! Old men weeping in the parks!
Moloch! Moloch! Nightmare of Moloch! Moloch the loveless! Mental Moloch! Moloch the heavy judger of men!

Moloch the incomprehensible prison! Moloch the crossbone soulless
jailhouse and Congress of sorrows! Moloch whose buildings are
judgement! Moloch the vast stone of war! Moloch the stunned
governments!
Moloch whose mind is pure machinery! Moloch whose blood is running
money! Moloch whose fingers are ten armies! Moloch whose
breast is a cannibal dynamo! Moloch whose ear is a smoking
tomb!
Moloch whose eyes are a thousand blind windows! Moloch whose
skyscrapers stand in the long streets like endless Jehovahs!
Moloch whose factories dream and croak in the fog! Moloch
whose smokestacks and antennae crown the cities!
Moloch whose love is endless oil and stone! Moloch whose soul is
electricity and banks! Moloch, whose poverty is the specter of
genius! Moloch whose fate is a cloud of sexless hydrogen! Moloch
whose name is the Mind!
Moloch in whom I sit lonely! Moloch in whom I dream Angels!
Crazy in Moloch! Cocksucker in Moloch! Lacklove and manless
in Moloch!
Moloch who entered my soul early! Moloch in whom I am a consciousness
without a body! Moloch who frightened me out of my natural
ecstasy! Moloch whom I abandon! Wake up in Moloch! Light
streaming out of the sky!
Moloch! Moloch! Robot apartments! invisible suburbs! skeleton
treasuries! blind capitals! demonic industries! spectral nations!
invincible madhouses! granite cocks! monstrous bombs!
They broke their backs lifting Moloch to Heaven! Pavements, trees,
radios, tons! lifting the city to Heaven which exists and is
everywhere about us!
Visions! omens! hallucinations! miracles! ecstasies! gone down the
American river!
Dreams! adorations! illuminations! religions! the whole boatload of
sensitive bullshit!
Breakthroughs! over the river! flips and crucifixions! gone down the
flood! Highs! Epiphanies! Despairs! Ten year's animal screams
and suicides! Minds! New loves! Mad generation! down on the
rocks of Time!
Real holy laughter in the river! They saw it all! the wild eyes! the holy
yells! They bade farewell! They jumped off the roof! to solitude!
waving! carrying flowers! Down to the river! into the street!

From: Allen Ginsberg, *Howl* (1956)

Annotations

1 **Moloch** ['məulɔk] in the Old Testament, a god to whom children were sacrificed; (fig.) a dreadful thing that requires sacrifice of human life, or causes destruction - 2 **to bash** to beat, smash - 9 **crossbone(s)** figure of two bones laid across each other, forming with the skull a conventional emblem of death - 20 **smokestack** chimney - 26 **cocksucker** (vulg.) G. "Schwanzlutscher", "Arschkriecher" - 26 **lacklove** lacking in love - 34 **cock** (vulg.) male sexual organ - 42 **flip** G. Hochwerfen einer Münze (beim Losen) - 43 **epiphany** [-'---] G. göttliche Erscheinung, Offenbarung

A) Understanding the Text

1. In this poem, "Moloch" is the name for a lot of things. Find some key expressions.
2. What does Ginsberg say about Moloch's mind, blood, fingers, breast, eyes, ear, soul, fate?
3. Translate some stanzas into German and try to hit the right tone.

B) Interpretation and Discussion

1. The poem sounds like a litany. Do you think it is a prayer, or do you think it is an accusation? What is the author's intention in making it look like a litany?
2. In the first and in the last stanza, Ginsberg repeatedly talks about, "they", "them". Who is meant by "they"?
3. In what way does the poem refer to "mass society" or "industrial society"?
4. Devise an over-all definition of what Ginsberg refers to by the expression "Moloch".
5. (a) Marcus Cunliffe calls the literature of the Beat Generation "repetitious and imprecise". As to Allen Ginsberg's poems, he writes,

   "There is a great deal of ferocity in it. Surrealist effects are aimed at. But there is more bad temper than indignation. It is a hit-and-miss poetry, a display of personality - and so a dangerously attractive kind of poetry for the legion of young Americans who want to be great writers but have no talent except the talent (temporary, alas) for being young."

   (Marcus Cunliffe, *The Literature of the United States,* (1954), Harmondsworth/England 1975, pp. 358f.)

   (b) George W. Lyon, Jr., offers a closer look at "Howl":

   "... Ginsberg identifies America as Hell, and 'Howl' is one of the most frightening explorations of Hell ever created. The sufferers Ginsberg shows us are the rebels, those who fight back by attempting to enjoy themselves, by attempting to make their lives meaningful, who find it impossible (this *is* Hell), and so end up most often in lonely hotelrooms, alone, annihilated, or in insane asylums. ... Ginsberg names Moloch, the false god, as the demon behind America's Hell. Moloch, the 'sphinx of cement and aluminum,' imprisons all of us, and if we are ever to enjoy any pure emotion, we must break out of Moloch's grasps, even if to do so we must commit suicide."

George W. Lyon, Jr., "Allen Ginsberg - Angel Headed Hipster", *Journal of Popular Culture,* Vol. III, Nr. 3/1969, p. 394.

Compare these two interpretations, their differences and similarities, and apply them to the text.

C) Language Work

Check up on the pronunciation of the following:

dynamo	hydrogen	granite
tomb	suburb	omen
antennae	demonic	hallucination
genius		crucifixion

D) Creative Writing

Write a similar litany - maybe in a satirical manner - on your teachers, on your school, on television, or on any subject of your own choice.

which abstract terms are correlated to which concrete terms?

Moloch, the false god, is the demon behind Am's cities

which is the true god?

dreams of living together in a community?

IV. Man and Nature

The 19th century pride in America's increasing industrial progress is clearly on the wane. Instead, a new affective as well as intellectual pattern has evolved: a nostalgic yearning for a simpler, essentially rural, and definitely more "virtuous" America. A renaissance of the idea that the cultivator of the soil is, of necessity, also a cultivator of virtue, is an easily discernible trend. There can be no doubt that the old proverb "The city for wealth, the country for health" has been rediscovered and that a new meaning has been added to the concept of "health". Its neo-romantic overtones reveal a truly sentimental dream of human possibilities under "untainted" conditions; such concepts indicate the omnipresence of those developments which tend to transform even the natural grandeur of the North American continent into a postindustrial wasteland.

Annotations

3 **on the wane** becoming less – 3 **affective** (psych.) emotional – 4 **to evolve** to develop gradually – 6 **to discern** [di'sə:n] to notice – 10 **untainted** unspoilt – 11 **omnipresent** present everywhere – 12 **grandeur** ['grændʒə] great beauty or power

1. Why I love her

"America, America, God shed his grace on thee..."

You ask me why I love her? Well, give me time and I'll explain.
Have you seen a Kansas sunset or an Arizona rain?
Have you drifted on a bayou down Louisiana way?
Have you watched the cold fog drifting over San Francisco Bay?

Have you heard a bobwhite calling in the Carolina pines
Or heard the bellow of a diesel in the Appalachia mines?
Does the call of the Niagara thrill you when you hear her waters roar?
Do you look with awe and wonder at her Massachusetts shore...
Where men, who braved a hard new world, first stepped on Plymouth's rock?
And do you think of them when you stroll along a New York City dock?

Have you seen a snowflake drifting in the Rockies... way up high?
Have you seen the sun come blazing down from a bright Nevada sky?
Do you hail to the Columbia as she rushes to the sea...
Or bow your head at Gettysburg... at our struggle to be free?

Have you seen the mighty Tetons?... Have you watched an eagle soar?
Have you seen the Mississippi roll along Missouri's shore?
Have you felt a chill at Michigan, when on a winter's day,
Her waters rage along the shore in thunderous display?
Does the word "Aloha"... make you warm? Do you stare in disbelief
When you see the surf come roaring in at Waimea Reef?

From Alaska's cold to the Everglades... from the Rio Grande to Maine ...
My heart cries out ... my pulse runs fast at the might of her domain.

You ask me why I love her?... I've a million reasons why.
My beautiful America... beneath God's wide, wide sky.

"And crown thy good with brotherhood
From sea to shining sea".

From: John Wayne, *"America, Why I love Her"*

Annotations

5 **bayou** ['baiu:] G. sumpfiger Flußarm – 7 **bobwhite** G. Wachtelart – 8 **bellow** roaring – 11 **Plymouth Rock** rock in Massachusetts on which the Pilgrim Fathers are said to have landed in 1620 – 14 **snowflake** snow crystal – 17 **Gettysburg** town in Pennsylvania, site of an important defeat of the Confederate forces, 1863, during the American Civil War – 18 **Tetons** ['ti:tnz] group of Rocky Mountain peaks in Wyoming – 18 **to soar** to sail in the air – 21 **display** G. Pracht – 23 **Waimea Reef** line of rocks off the Hawaiian coast – 24 **Everglades** swampy, partly forested region in Florida – 25 **domain** lands

A) Understanding the Text

1. By way of answering the question why he loves America Wayne says "give me time and I'll explain" (line 3), and at the end he says "I've a million reasons why" (line 26). What are the actual reasons he gives?
2. Locate the places that Wayne mentions on a map of the USA.

B) Interpretation and Discussion

1. Instead of making statements about why he loves America Wayne asks questions. Why?
2. What kind of response do these questions aim at?
3. Can you group together the items which Wayne mentions under some headings?
4. What is it that Wayne loves about America? Does he really have a million reasons?

5. Suppose you met a patriotic American at the end of your tour through America. Which of these questions might he ask you, the tourist, and which not? Give reasons.
6. The rain in Arizona is probably as wet as anywhere. Yet in Wayne's song it takes on some special quality. How is that to be explained? Analyze the verbal signals.

2. Bob Greene, It's No Longer John Wayne's America

There are no answers to this. Now that it is with us, we probably will live with it forever. The line in the airport concourse is stretching for 30 feet, hardly moving, but everyone is waiting patiently. No one is angry. Up against the wall over there, a businessman is being frisked. He looks at his watch while it happens, wanting to be sure he does not miss his plane. No one glances back at him as they walk past.

Another man walks through a big metal-detecting shed. Apparently he does not pass the test, for he too is told to wait. A uniformed security policeman approaches, holding an electric cattleprod-like device with a long metal loop on the end. The security policeman sticks the device under the man's arms, between the man's legs, inside the man's suit jacket. No one stops to watch.

In the end it is not the big events of history by which we remember our times, not the presidential elections or World Series that we flash back to when we try to remember a time in our lives. Those are just guideposts. Rather, it is the little parts of life, the things we deal with every day without noticing or thinking, that come back to us later to remind us what it was like. And when we think back to this part of our times, the image that may haunt us most is that of an airport, any airport, and of the citizens of the United States of America being frisked and searched and poked at and funneled through electronic mazes. All of them presumed innocent, but all of them also suspected of the possibility of harboring a secret madness.

Of course it has to be this way. Of course with things as sick as they are in the land it is absolutely essential that this has happened. Of course, ugly as it is to watch and be part of, there is no real alternative, and it must be done.

But knowing that does not make it any better. Finally we are beginning to realize that so many of our beliefs about the openness and warmth and fundamental goodness of this country are turning out to be myths. The new airport scenes say it for us: We are afraid of each other, we are terrified of the evil that may lie inside our neighbor's heart, we cannot afford to be trusting anymore. We do not and cannot accept the sanity of strangers on faith. We want everyone to be searched, including ourselves. It makes us feel better.

All the American children who are growing up now, who have yet to take their first airplane ride, will never know it was ever any other way. They will not know of the days when a person carried a shopping bag full of gifts onto an airplane with just a nod and a smile to the stewardess. They will not know of wandering around an airport as if it were a public library or a ballpark or an art museum, an open, cheerful place instead of a hall of suspicion and fear.

On some flights, one of the selections on the stereo headsets is a series of spoken-word essays from an album by John Wayne entitled "America, Why I Love Her". Over a background of inspiring, patriotic music, Wayne talks about what he calls "the good things". He says, "We hear a lot about war, the hurricanes that hit our shore, but all that does is sing the blues about America. What about the good things, the men who love their wives and take their sons fishing?" He says, "In my son's eye, I spotted a gleam. 'I wanted to surprise you, dad - I'm on the football team.'" He says, "You ask why I love America; give me the time and I'll explain. Have you seen a Kansas sunset, or a Louisiana rain? Have you strolled along a New York dock? Have you seen the mighty Tetons? Have you watched an eagle soar?" But the airplane's captain cuts in and says, "Sorry for that delay in taking off, but we had to wait a while due to airport security, which unfortunately is all too necessary these days."

It would be so nice if John Wayne's America were still the real America. But it isn't, and pretending that the most striking thing about the United States is still its open skies and beautiful scenery isn't enough, not in a time of grayness and distrust and fear and noises behind you in the airport ticket line. If the mighty Tetons and the soaring eagle are the symbols of John Wayne's America, then the terrible, necessary scene inside the airports is the truest symbol of the new America. Strangers searching through our bags and feeling at our clothing do not seem to bother us much: that kind of privacy is just another principle that we have had to give up, another trade made inevitable to deal with the terrors of our time.

From: *San Francisco Sunday Examiner & Chronicle,* April 8, 1979, p. 4

Annotations

3 **line** BE queue - 3 **concourse** hall (in airport or railroad terminal) where crowds gather - 5 **to frisk** to search a person, G. "filzen" - 10 **cattle-prod** G. Stab zum Antreiben des Viehs - 14 **World Series** US baseball championship games - 14 **to flash back to** quickly turn the mind to some past event - 20 **to poke at s.o.** to push (fingers, pointed object) into s.o. - 20 **to funnel** to pass (a crowd etc.) through a narrow space (**funnel** G. Trichter) - 21 **maze** G. Irrgarten - 22 **to harbor** to keep (thoughts, feelings) in the mind - 31 **sanity** mental health - 31 **on faith** confidently - 37 **ballpark** baseball ground - 40 **headset** G. Kopfhörer

A) Understanding the Text

1. In the first two paragraphs Greene describes scenes that have become a familiar sight not only in American airports. What kind of scenes are these?
2. What, according to Greene, are the things what we tend to remember historical periods by?
3. What is the image he will remember most vividly?
4. How does he contrast the relationship between people in modern American society and their traditional beliefs?
5. Where does Greene see the main difference between John Wayne's America and today's reality?
6. What is his view of what he calls "Wayne's America"?

B) Interpretation and Discussion

1. Do you think such an enormous amount of security in airports is necessary these days? Why? Why not?
2. Greene calls airport security "the truest symbol of the new America" and the "mighty Tetons" (very high mountains in Wyoming) and "the searing eagle" the symbols of John Wayne's America. Can you describe the contrast suggested by this kind of symbolism?
3. What is Greene's basic attitude towards the lyrics of John Wayne's songs?
4. Greene characterizes modern society with the words grayness, distrust, fear, noise, terror. Look for the antonyms in John Wayne's poems.

C) Language Work

1. The description of the airport in the first two paragraphs is in the Present Tense. Would it make any difference if you re-wrote these passages in the Past Tense?
2. Make a list of the features of American life that Bob Greene criticizes. Now formulate these criticisms as a nostalgic American might, starting with "I wish...", "If only..." or "America could be such a beautiful country if. . ." (e.g. I wish people would stop to watch).
3. Make these words negative by adding *un–, in–* or *dis–*.

satisfied	equal	appoint	obey
fortunate	equality	comfort	applicable
favourable	order	comfortable	efficient

D) Creative Writing

Write an essay on the similarities and/or differences between Jack Anderson's, John Wayne's and Bob Greene's America, and express your attitude towards the respective validity of each author's view.

He did not give up his farm for a new road and Grant Grimsey

3. Death of a Yankee: A Man Who Fought Progress and Lost

by Nancy Shulins

ASCUTNEY, Vt. - The flames were hot enough to melt the blue plastic bubble on a police cruiser parked nearby.

The people watched and waited, hoping they'd see him stumble out of the woods or emerge from the barn, charred and dusty and mad as hell, waving his fist at the bulldozers and trucks.

But when the old man's dogs tried to dig their way into the burning farmhouse, the people knew.

No need to wait for the verdict, nor read the fire marshal's report. He'd warned them.

"I was born here and I'll die here," he'd vowed throughout that long, hot summer.

His neighbors wandered home, shaking their heads and shielding their eyes from the eerie glow that lit the village.

Romaine Tenney, 64, as stubborn a Yankee as God ever made, had tried to fight an army of bulldozers with a pitchfork. When he saw he couldn't win, he did what he had to.

He died where he was born.

Today, 15 years later, regulars at Ascutney's general store still talk of Old Man Tenney and the summer the bulldozers chewed through the hill, clearing the way for Interstate 91.

For the tourists who speed past the southeastern Vermont village, Ascutney is just another cloverleaf on the journey north. No monument tells them that inches below the pavement an old man's home and life lie buried.

The thunder of bulldozers and heavy trucks began at sunrise and continued until dark, as the ribbon of dirt that would become I-91 inched northward through Vermont that summer.

It was 1964. People did not denounce progress - they made way for it.

Ascutney did its part. Its few hundred souls stepped around the equipment and conversed over the roar of machinery that became a soundtrack for the summer.

And the cries of an old man fighting to save his birthplace were lost in the din.

Today, his sister-in-law Peggy and others who knew the village as it was then still talk of Old Man Tenney. This is what they remember.

The 75-acre farm was already 78 years old when Myron Tenney bought it in 1892, the year he and his bride boarded their horse-drawn sleigh for the treacherous trip down from Mendon Mountain.

It was on the Ascutney hillside where the Tenneys raised their nine children, and where Romaine Tenney was born.

As years passed, the others moved away. Romaine, a bachelor, stayed on with four dogs, three cats, two horses and 20 cows. Only World War II took him away from home.

He farmed with horses and hayed with a pitchfork. He would not drive a car, his hatred for engines was too great.

By the time it was finished, 22 years after it began, I-91 would measure 178 miles in Vermont, opening the way for continuous travel from New Haven, Conn., to the Quebec border.

It would replace old, winding Route 5, a move state officials said would reduce accidents along a major traffic corridor.

And it would meet Route 31 in Ascutney, in a cloverleaf that would bisect Old Man Tenney's place.

From the start, the construction equipment rankled the strapping Vermonter, whose bushy beard rested on the bib of his overalls and flapped when he talked.

At first, he complained about the bulldozers in the same off-hand way he cursed his arthritis, electricity and daylight-saving time.

His first line of defense was to ignore them.

For a while, he went about his chores as though the machines weren't there, as though the trucks weren't creeping closer to his house, tearing up his fields and using his dooryard as a roadway.

The state people who came to see him used words he didn't understand. Old Man Tenney didn't know what eminent domain meant. But whatever it was, he was having none of it.

In June 1964, they offered him $10,600 for his property, and he shook his head.

Once he'd split the money with his eight brothers and sisters, the state's offer would have left the old farmer with just over $1,000 in his pocket. Not much to start life over with at age 64.

Two months later, a Woodstock court jury upped the figure to $13,600. Still, the old man refused.

On Friday, Sept. 11, the sheriff came with a court order to remove Romaine Tenney's possessions and he brought along four helpers and two trucks to get the job done.

The old man watched as the small crew went to work in his shed, taking out the old tools and harness and piling them on a knoll a hundred yards away.

That night, Emerson and Peggy Tenney dropped in on the old man. At his request, they took him to Claremont to do his shopping.

Later, he unpacked his provisions and bade his brother and sister-in-law good night, assuring them he had what he needed.

Howard Fitch of Ascutney drove his babysitter home that night, a trip that would take him past Old Man Tenney's place.

It was on his way home that Fitch noticed something was wrong. The interior of the house emitted a strange glow. So did the barn. And so did the pile of tools and harnesses stacked on the knoll.

Fitch raced to the fire station and pulled the alarm. But the men who reported to the scene could do little more than round up the farm animals that wandered aimlessly through the fields and to keep the flames from spreading to the hillside.

When the smoke cleared, officials began sifting through the ashes. Days later, they found what they were looking for. On Sept. 23, a memorial service was held for Romaine Tenney.

Fifteen years later, Peggy Tenney climbs the uneven terrain of the Ascutney hillside, pulling her coat more tightly around her stocky frame to ward off the late afternoon chill.

From her vantage point, she watches the traffic that spills from the off-ramp of the highway below.

A pile of bricks is barely visible in the brush, but she knows just where to look for the remains of the old man's shed.

"That's where he stored the sleigh," she says, stooping to pick up one of the old bricks. "He loved that sleigh – he used to spend hours polishing it, painting it.

"It's not hard to understand why he did what he did. He couldn't part with any of it – it was his life."

Mrs. Tenney remembers the letter the state sent her six months after the fire, outlining plans for a memorial to her brother-in-law.

The marker was forgotten, and the Tenney Road sign erected shortly after was stolen by vandals.

But there's something else that bothers Peggy Tenney, she says.

"Nobody ever said they were sorry."

From: *San Francisco Sunday Examiner & Chronicle,* May 20, 1979, p. 16

Annotations

3 **Vt.** Vermont [və:'mɔnt], New England state in the Northeast – 4 **cruiser** ['kru:zə] (here:) police car – 6 **charred** blackened by ashes – 6 **mad as hell** (coll.) very angry – 10 **verdict** G. Untersuchungsergebnis – 15 **eerie** causing fear – 17 **pitchfork** G. Heu-, Mistgabel – 20 **regular** a r. customer – 24 **cloverleaf** G. (kleeblattförmiges) Autobahnkreuz – 29 **to denounce** to speak against – 34 **din** loud and unpleasant noise – 38 **to board** to get on or into – 38 **sleigh** [slei] G. Pferdeschlitten – 49 **Conn.** Connecticut [kə'netikət], New England state – 57 **to bisect** [bai'sekt] to divide into two parts – 54 **to rankle** to cause bitterness in – 54 **strapping** big and strong – 55 **bib** G. Brustlatz – 55 **to flap** to wave up and down – 57 **off-hand** careless – 60 **chore** daily necessary job (in house, on farm) – 64 **eminent domain** G. Enteignungsrecht – 65 **having none of** (coll.) not accepting – 71 **to up** to raise – 77 **knoll** [nəul] small round hill – 85 **to emit** to send out (light, sound, smoke) – 86 **to stack** to pile up – 87 **to report to** (here:) to go to – 88 **to round up** to gather together (cattle) – 91 **to sift through** to make a close examination of

– 92 **memorial service** G. Gedenkgottesdienst – 95 **stocky frame** G. stämmige Gestalt – 97 **vantage point** G. Aussichtspunkt – 97 **to spill** to flow off – 97 **off-ramp** G. Autobahnausfahrt – 99 **brush** (land covered by) small rough trees and bushes

A) Understanding the Text

1. Gather all information on the village of Ascutney where Tenney lived.
2. What did Old Man Tenney's life look like? Where did he live, what was his job, etc.?
3. Give a short account of the controversy between Tenney and the State of Vermont. What was it all about?
4. How did the authorities justify the construction of the new Interstate 91?
5. What happened to Tenney and his farm after the sheriff had removed his possessions?
6. How did the authorities react towards Old Man Tenney's death?

B) Interpretation and Discussion

1. Why wouldn't Tenney give up his farm? What are the psychological reasons behind his attitude?
2. What do you think of the way the state authorities handled the case, before and after Tenney's death?
3. Who is to blame for Old Man Tenney's tragic death
   - his family who didn't help him?
   - the state authorities who insisted on an expropriation?
   - the court that ordered his possessions to be removed?
   - the sheriff who enforced the order?
   - the people of Ascutney who did not care about the problem?
   - Old Man Tenney himself because he was opposed to any kind of change?
4. Do you agree with the reasons for a new Interstate as they are given by the authorities?
5. Do you hold the view that freeways are absolutely necessary in our industrialized society?
6. "It was 1964. People did not denounce progress – they made way for it." Compare the significance of progress in Old Man Tenney's time with contemporary attitudes towards unlimited progress.

C) Language Work

1. Here are some words from the above text which are exclusively or mainly American: police cruiser, mad (= angry), truck, fire marshal, cloverleaf, dooryard, sheriff, highway. Also, the spelling of 'neighbor'

and 'defense' are American, as is the use of 'northward' instead of 'northwards'.

Which of the following words are American, which British English? Consult your dictionary to find out.

mailbox - letter-box; cookie - biscuit; petrol - gasoline; Foreign Office - State Department; to shine shoes - to polish shoes; rock - stone; lift - elevator

2. How does the pronunciation in British and American English differ in these words:

   clerk, advertisement, schedule, secretary, (the letter) 'z', tomato, dictionary

3. Two statements or ideas can be contrasted by means of various adverbs or phrases, e.g. although, though, even though, while, whereas, in spite of (the fact that), for (all), notwithstanding, yet, however, but, nevertheless, all the same, still, even so, adjective or adverb + as/though (e.g. Strange as it may seem...), no matter

   Use these expressions in contrasting the following statements; change the wording where necessary.

   The people watched and waited for a long time. The old man did not emerge from the burning farmhouse.

   Old Man Tenney bravely fought the bulldozers. He lost in the end.

   Tenney has been dead for many years now. The regulars at Ascutney's general store still talk of him.

   Modern engines make farming easier. Tenney farmed with horses and hayed with a pitchfork.

   In June 1964 they offered him $ 10,600 for his property. He shook his head.

   Fitch immediately raced to the fire station. They could do little more than keep the flames from spreading to the hillside.

4. "Highways bury good crop land" "Highways make farms more productive"

"Highways bury good crop land."

"Highways make farms more productive."

One worries about "paving the world." Another sees roads fulfilling the promise of fresh, varied, lower-cost food. Who's right?

Highways do take land out of production. 10 acres of right-of-way for each 2-lane mile. 25 acres for an Interstate mile. Interchange right-of-way can take 50 to 100 acres. An acre can yield 150 bushels of corn, wheat for 1,600 loaves of bread. In a world of population growth, increasing competition for food and livelihood, understandably some people might ask "Can we afford the luxury of these super roads?"

Others talk of roads as a productive tool increasing farm yields. Bringing farmers fuel, fertilizer, insecticides, seeds and machinery. Transporting crops and livestock to market. Rushing perishable fruits, vegetables, eggs, to processors and consumers. Moving grain to storage and shipping points. Lowering food prices by lowering transportation costs. Improving variety and quality in grocery stores. Farmers say, "Good roads help keep production up and the transportation costs down."

Highways and streets, city and country, take less than 1% of our total land area. Road miles have increased only 18% since 1930. Mostly in suburbs. Traffic, meanwhile, increased 50% the past decade. 70% for trucks! Result: heavy travel, roads wearing twice as fast as they are being replaced—a problem accelerated by construction costs doubling every decade. Roads bring us our food. And most other things in our lives. That's why we need programs to maintain and improve our highway asset.

Caterpillar equipment is used to build and maintain roads and power trucks. We believe America's well being rides on our roads.

There are no simple solutions. Only intelligent choices.

CATERPILLAR

Caterpillar, Cat and ⊞ are Trademarks of Caterpillar Tractor Co.

Annotations

6 **acre** G. Morgen, ca. 4000 m² – 6 **right-of-way** G. zu öffentlichen Zwecken enteignetes Gelände – 7 **lane** G. Fahrspur – 8 **interstate (highway)** G. Fernstraße – 8 **interchange** G. (Straßen)Anschlußstelle – 11 **bushel** [-u-] ca. 35 liters – 20 **fertilizer** G. Dünger – 21 **insecticide** chemical substance made to kill insects – 22 **livestock** farm animals – 23 **perishable** G. leichtverderblich – 24 **to process** to treat and preserve (food) by a particular process – 43 **to accelerate** to cause to move, or develop, faster – 49 **asset** valuable quality

A) Understanding the Text

1. What are the drawbacks of the development of the transportation system?
2. In what ways will a farmer benefit from improved transportation systems?
3. The language of the advertisement is highly charged with technical and statistical details. Summarize the general information value of those details.

B) Interpretation and Discussion

1. Do you agree with the conclusion that "America's well being rides on our roads"? Well being is equated with material progress. Can you think of alternative definitions of a nation's well being?
2. This is an advertisement for road building equipment. Is it not strange that it does not emphasize the specific qualities of *Caterpillar* products? What is the major purpose of this advertisement?
3. The environmental debate has been raging for several years. Does this advertisement contribute "intelligent choices" as its authors maintain?

C) Creative Writing

1. Compose an advertisement for the conservation movement.
2. Compose an advertisement for *Caterpillar* which emphasizes the qualities of road-building equipment.
3. Use the visual materials of this advertisement in order to compose an ad for other products or services.

5. A note on the camping craze that is currently sweeping America

by Richard Brautigan

As much as anything else, the Coleman lantern is the symbol of the camping craze that is currently sweeping America, with its unholy white light burning in the forests of America!

Last summer, a Mr. Norris was drinking at a bar in San Francisco. It was Sunday night and he'd had six or seven. Turning to the guy on the next stool, he said, "What are you up to?"

"Just having a few," the guy said.

"That's what I'm doing," Mr. Norris said. "I like it."

"I know what you mean," the guy said. "I had to lay off for a couple of years. I'm just starting up again."

"What was wrong?" Mr. Norris said.

"I had a hole in my liver," the guy said.

"In your liver?"

"Yeah, the doctor said it was big enough to wave a flag in. It's better now. I can have a couple once in a while. I'm not supposed to, but it won't kill me."

"Well, I'm thirty-two years old," Mr. Norris said. "I've had three wives and I can't remember the names of my children."

The guy on the next stool, like a bird on the next island, took a sip from his Scotch and soda. The guy liked the sound of the alcohol in his drink. He put the glass back on the bar.

"That's no problem," he said to Mr. Norris. "The best thing I know for remembering the names of children from previous marriages, is to go out camping, try a little trout fishing. Trout fishing is one of the best things in the world for remembering children's names."

"Is that right?" Mr. Norris said.

"Yeah," the guy said.

"That sounds like an idea," Mr Norris said. "I've got to do something. Sometimes I think one of them is named Carl, but that's impossible. My third-ex hated the name Carl."

"You try some camping and that trout fishing," the guy on the next stool said. "And you'll remember the names of your unborn children."

"Carl! Carl! Your mother wants you!" Mr. Norris yelled as a kind of joke, then he realized that it wasn't very funny. He was getting there.

He'd had a couple more and then his head would always fall forward and hit the bar like a gunshot. He'd always miss his glass, so he wouldn't cut his face. His head would always jump up and look startled around the bar, people staring at it. He'd get up then, and take it home.

The next morning Mr. Norris went down to a sporting goods store and charged his equipment. He charged a 9 x 9 foot dry finish tent with an aluminum center pole. Then he charged an Arctic sleeping bag filled with eiderdown and an air mattress and an air pillow to go with the sleeping bag. He also charged an air alarm clock to go along with the idea of night and waking in the morning.

He charged a two-burner Coleman stove and a Coleman lantern and a folding aluminum table and a big set of interlocking aluminum cookware and a portable ice box.

The last thing he charged were his fishing tackle and a bottle of insect repellent.

He left the next day for the mountains.

Hours later, when he arrived in the mountains, the first sixteen campgrounds he stopped at were filled with people. He was a little surprised. He had no idea the mountains would be so crowded.

At the seventeenth campground, a man had just died of a heart attack and the ambulance attendants were taking down his tent. They lowered the center pole and then pulled up the corner stakes. They folded the tent neatly and put it in the back of the ambulance, right beside the man's body. They drove off down the road, leaving behind them in the air, a cloud of brilliant white dust. The dust looked like the light from a Coleman lantern.

Mr. Norris pitched his tent right there and set up all his equipment and soon had it all going at once. After he finished eating a dehydrated beef Stroganoff dinner, he turned off all his equipment with the master air switch and went to sleep, for it was now dark.

It was about midnight when they brought the body and placed it beside the tent, less than a foot away from where Mr. Norris was sleeping in his Arctic sleeping bag.

He was awakened when they brought the body. They weren't exactly the quietest body bringers in the world. Mr. Norris could see the bulge of the body against the side of the tent. The only thing that separated him from the dead body was a thin layer of 6 oz. water resistant and mildew resistant DRY FINISH green AMERIFLEX poplin.

Mr. Norris un-zipped his sleeping bag and went outside with a gigantic hound-like flashlight. He saw the body bringers walking down the path toward the creek.

"Hey, you guys!" Mr. Norris shouted. "Come back here. You forgot something."

"What do you mean?" one of them said. They both looked very sheepish, caught in the teeth of the flashlight.

"You know what I mean," Mr. Norris said. "Right now!"

The body bringers shrugged their shoulders, looked at each other and then reluctantly went back, dragging their feet like children all the way. They picked up the body. It was heavy and one of them had trouble getting hold of the feet.

That one said, kind of hopelessly to Mr. Norris, "You won't change your mind?"

"Goodnight and good-bye," Mr Norris said.

They went off down the path toward the creek, carrying the body between them. Mr. Norris turned his flashlight off and he could hear them, stumbling over the rocks along the bank of the creek. He could hear them swearing at each other. He heard one of them say, "Hold your end up." Then he couldn't hear anything.

About ten minutes later he saw all sorts of lights go on at another campsite down along the creek. He heard a distant voice shouting, "The answer is no! You already woke up the kids. They have to have their rest. We're going on a four-mile hike tomorrow up to Fish Konk Lake. Try someplace else."

From: Richard Brautigan, *Trout Fishing in America,* New York, Dell Publishing Co. (Copyright Richard Brautigan, 1967)

Annotations

4 **Coleman lantern** G. Campinglampe – 10 **to have a few** (coll.) to take several alcoholic drinks – 36 **to get there** (here:) to become drunk – 42 **to charge s.th.** G. anschreiben lassen; Ware gegen Vorlage einer Scheckkarte mitnehmen – 42 **dry finish tent** G. Zelt mit Trockenimprägnierung – 43 **aluminum** [əˈluːminəm] BE aluminium [æljuˈminjəm] – 48 **interlocking cookware** G. Kochtöpfe, die man ineinanderstellen kann – 58 **corner stakes** Zeltheringe – 63 **dehydrated** [ˌdiːhaiˈdreitid] G. durch Wasserentzug getrocknet – 72 **6 oz** 6 ounces, ca. 170 g. – 72 **mildew resistant** G. nicht schimmelnd – 73 **poplin** G. Popelin(stoff)

A) Understanding the Text

1. This text can be divided into several parts, each of them dealing with another topic. How many units can you find? Sum up their contents in two or three sentences of your own.
2. What are Mr. Norris's reasons for going camping?
3. How does he prepare for the trip?
4. Describe what happens after he arrives in the mountains.

B) Interpretation and Discussion

1. In Brautigan's story, nobody wants to accept the dead body that has been dropped beside the tent. Does this show
   - that people are selfish?
   - that they don't care for each other?
   - that there is no space left for the body?
   - that everybody is frightened by death?

   Discuss the alternatives.
2. In our time, leisure time activities are getting more and more important, even for industry and business. Discuss what the second part of the story has to do with the commercial exploitation of people's needs.
3. Critics view the story as a satire on either
   a) the over-estimated value of outdoor recreation
   or b) the commercialization of people's need of vacations,
   or c) the modern form of mass tourism.

   Discuss these statements and refer them to the text.

C) Language Work

a) Vocabulary

1. Can you find other words for *craze,* as in "this is the latest craze in pop music"?

2. "My *third-ex* hated the name Carl." What is meant by this?
3. Make a list of things, actions, expressions that have something to do with bars and drinking. Draw on your own experiences and use a dictionary.
4. Make a list of the things you would need for a camping holiday.
5. Explain the form and function of a *flash light,* a *tent,* a *zip.* Try not to use your hands.
6. What do a *hike,* a *walk* and a *march* have in common, and how do they differ?
7. If something is *portable* you can carry it. What about *visible, audible, tangible, edible, inhabitable, legible, soluble, pardonable, navigable?*

b) Phrasal verbs

Find out the meaning of the following phrasal verbs and use them in sentences of your own.

to be up to (something, no good, etc.)
to lay off (drinking, cigarettes, etc.)
to start up (in some career)
to go with (e.g. Her lipstick doesn't go with her blouse.)
to take down (a tent, etc.)
to pull up (the corner stakes, etc.)
to turn off (the light, etc.)

D) Creative Writing

1. Find suitable topics for which to compose sentences on the following lines:
   (a) As long a sentence as possible, which is still grammatical and acceptable.
   (b) A series of short separate sentences.
   (c) A sequence in which narrative and speech are rapidly alternated.
   (d) A series of sentences marked by strong contrasts.
2. Write an account of an unexpected meeting and conversation between yourself and one of the following:
   - Noan;
   - A visitor from another planet
   - Your great-grandfather
3. Make up a script for a TV commercial in which a mail-order company advertises equipment for deep-sea diving / a safari / a boat-trip down the Mississippi.
4. Imagine two strangers meeting in a bar and the conversation they might start. Describe the scene.

Drawing by Ed Fisher; © 1979 The New Yorker Magazine, Inc.

wilderness wild uncultivated land with no sign of human presence – **to spoil** to ruin – **irretrievable** that cannot be put back into the original better state

Discussion

Analyze the impact of mass leisure activities on the environment and discuss possible solutions of the problems.

6. Come to where the flavor is. Come to Marlboro Country.

A) Understanding the Advertisement

1. Come to where the sun is. – Come to where happiness is. – Come to where the flavor is.

   Compare these three sentences.

   (a) Can you think of contexts where each of them makes sense?

   (b) Is there a place "where the flavor is"?

2. Where is Marlboro Country?
3. The picture in this advertisement shows what is called "Marlboro Country". Describe what it looks like.

B) Interpretation and Discussion

1. What do you associate, what comes to your mind, when you just look at the picture?
2. You can find Marlboro advertisements especially in magazines like *Playboy, Newsweek, Time,* etc., which are mainly read by, and cater to, people who live in cities. What does their environment look like, and what does Marlboro promise them?
3. Compare the world in this advertisement with the world as it is depicted in the Chester Himes and Allen Ginsberg texts.
4. Marlboro adds a special value to the flavor of their cigarettes. "The higher meaning of this Marlboro Man and the wilderness he faces down cannot be written in terms of tobacco. Not cigarettes but metaphors ... are being merchandised."
   (Bruce A. Lohof, "The Higher Meaning of Marlboro Cigarettes," *Journal of Popular Culture,* vol. III, Nr. 3/1969, p. 447)
   What does Lohof mean by "metaphor"?

V. The New Greening of the American Dream

The loss of the "American Dream"-security (which also served the functions of a secularized religion) has led to an increasing number of new creeds, 'ersatz'-cults, and reformulations of a better future. Americans have either withdrawn from their sordid reality or devoted themselves to the formulation of new "life styles", "philosophies", and "cultural patterns". They all pay lip service to "radical changes", but, in fact, almost all of them fall back on the essentials of the American Dream: the belief in a better future, in harmonious social organization of morally superior human – and specifically American – beings. Charles Reich's romanticized "consciousness III" is a perfect example of this catering to the need-, value- and expectation system which has experienced the bitter dissonance between dream and reality.

Annotations

3 **to secularize** to remove from the control of the church – 5 **sordid** base, vile, poor – 7 **to pay lip service to** to support in words, but not in fact – 10 **Charles Reich** see "The Greening of America" p. 74 – 11 **to cater to** to aim to satisfy (needs etc.)

1. Yearns for 1776 Spirit

Dear Editor,

As I see the United States slowly crumble from the effects of the policies of government, it is time for me as an American to ask, "When will things really change?"

When will the monetary system, over which the government so cleverly took control in a period of 150 years, stop printing worthless bills to cover its deficits while at the same time putting available credit out of the reach of individuals?

When will the theft of my money in the name of taxes stop? When will this money, taken from me, stop being given to those who refuse to work because government makes it more profitable for them not to?

When will government stop supporting countries that don't appreciate me, and even despise me because I'm an American?

When will government tell us the real cause of inflation and stop blaming it on private industry?

When will politicians stop implementing short-term schemes that promise me something for nothing to capture my vote?

I am an individual, with individual problems, and it is clear to me now that government cannot solve my problems, but only make them worse. It is time for America to stop hiding behind the mask of majority rule, political slogans, and the idea that government will take care of us.

It is time for Americans to recapture the spirit that set us free over 200 years ago, and remember the reason for which we originally sought freedom. I realize I am only one. But still I am one. For there to be waves, there must first be ripples. I cannot do everything, but still I will not refuse to do something.

John Doe, Chicago

Annotations

1 **to yearn for** [jə:n] to have a strong desire – 2 **to crumble** to break into (very small) pieces – 5 **monetary** of money – 9 **theft** stealing – 16 **to implement** to put into practice – 16 **short-term** G. kurzfristig – 16 **scheme** [ski:m] (dishonest) plan of action – 17 **to capture** to gain – 25 **ripple** very small wave

A) Understanding the Text

1. Name the major reasons for the sense of discontent.
2. Use the negative aspects of life in contemporary America in order to construe the essence of its positive alternative – "the spirit of 1776".
3. The last paragraph seems to indicate a belief in the changeability of the system. Who should be the agents of this change?

B) Interpretation and Discussion

1. The letter calls taxes "the theft of my money". Do you agree with this view? Discuss the pros and cons of tax reduction or tax increase.
2. The letter refers to "anti-Americanism". What could be the material and psychological reasons for this attitude in different countries? What is your attitude towards the U.S., who or what has shaped your views?
3. The writer yearns for the "golden past". Do you think that 200 years ago the situation of the individual was better than it seems to be today?

human values more than material values

2. People Are Looking Inward, Away from Material Possessions

by Louis Harris

Although most Americans are increasingly absorbed in coping with the problems of inflation and energy in their daily lives, there is evidence that their deeper desires don't involve the acquisition of physical goods. Indications are that this country is in a post-industrial, non-materialistic era. By 89-9 percent, Americans say they are seeking "experiences that make you peaceful inside."

By 91-7 percent, an overwhelming majority reports wanting to use their own creative abilities. One concern people express about this age of explosive technological breakthrough is that it will result in a push-button society, where many of the functions of life are handled almost automatically. As more technology has been introduced, Americans have expressed an increasing desire to have ample opportunities to use their creative talents. By 81-14 percent, most Americans say they "want to be involved in efforts where people cooperate rather than compete." When public opinion has swung heavily toward favoring the deregulation of business, accompanied by more direct competition, Americans apparently want less competition in their private lives.

By 72-24 percent, a majority chooses "breaking up big things and getting back to more humanized living," instead of "developing bigger and more efficient ways of doing things." Although most Americans acknowledge that bigger organizations tend to be more efficient and technologically advanced, people are apprehensive about human values being sacrificed in the push for efficiency. People would like to see more competition among smaller organizations, even if this results in some inefficiencies. The rationalization is that it might enhance the status of "humanized living."

On weighing the need for more jobs and products on the one hand, and a better non-material existence on the other, most Americans choose fewer product acquisitions.

By 53-40 percent, a majority rejects putting more emphasis on "satisfying our needs for goods and services" and instead gives a higher priority to "learning to get our pleasure out of non-material things."

By 55-40 percent, a majority would choose to emphasize "learning to appreciate human values more than material values" than "finding ways to create more jobs for producing more goods." Two years ago, however, a 63-29 percent majority agreed. Although the number has declined since 1977, a majority still givs higher priority to non-material values.

From: *San Francisco Examiner,* May 18, 1979

Annotations

4 **to cope with** to deal successfully with – 25 **apprehensive** worried – 28 **enhance** to increase – 33 **priority** G. Vorrang

A) Understanding the Text

1. Recall the fundamental change in attitude in contemporary Americans as it is reported by Louis Harris.
2. What seems to be the reason for the increasing desire to use one's own creative talents?
3. Collect the statements made in the text about a majority of Americans, and compare them with each other. Do they all point in the same direction?

B) Interpretation and Discussion

1. 89 percent of the Americans are seeking "experiences that make you peaceful inside". What could be the experiences that make them think so?
2. If 81 percent want to cooperate rather than compete, can you imagine the role competition plays in their lives?
3. What is the meaning of a "more humanized life"? What has to be changed in order to make life more humane?
4. Make a list of "human" and another one of "material values". Do you think people might really change their materialistic attitudes? If so, under what conditions?

C) Language Work

Choose the word or phrase which is closest in meaning to the one in italics.

1. Bigger organizations tend to be more *efficient.*
   a) powerful b) effective c) productive d) wealthy
2. Given the choice, most Americans choose fewer *product acquisitions.*
   a) purchases of goods b) shopping opportunities
   c) means of production d) brands of products
3. Most Americans are *absorbed with* the problems of daily life.
   a) worried about b) occupied by c) interested in
   d) shocked at
4. Americans *apparently* want less competition.
   a) probably b) usually c) definitely d) of course

use technology to gain individual freedom

3. The Greening of America

by Charles Reich

Today we are witnesses to a great moment in history: a turn from the pessimism that has closed in on modern industrial society; the rebirth of a future; the rebirth of people in a sterile land. If that process had to be summed up in a single word, that word would be freedom. Freedom from outmoded economic and political doctrines, freedom from oppressive institutions, freedom from the San Quentin consciousness by which we lock the doors of our minds. Freedom that is expressed in every metaphor of the new consciousness, long hair, a new way of walking, the ocean and the open road. But freedom is incredibly complex in a complex society.
We are only beginning to realize the incredible vastness of the changes that are coming. Most views of what is happening are woefully inadequate.

Liberals can only imagine another stage of reform, a rearranging of priorities, a revitalization of the bill of rights. Many blacks, and many spokesmen for the poor, cannot see much beyond the issues of social justice and the end of domination by one culture. The New Left is still playing out the battle against capitalism and imperialism. But if we think of all that is now challenged – the nature of education, the very validity of institutionalism and the legal system, the nature and purposes of work, the course of man's dealing with environment, the relationship of self to technology and society – we can see that the present transformation goes beyond anything in modern history.

But choice of a life style is not peripheral, it is the heart of the new awakening. What is coming is nothing less than a new way of life and a new man – a man with renewed energies and imagination – a man who is part of the living world.

What happened to the American people? In a word, powerlessness. We lost the ability to control our lives or our society because we had placed ourselves excessively under the domination of the market and technology. Finally we totally abandoned ourselves to the Corporate State, cutting ourselves off from our sources and our consciousness to such an extent that we were threatened with destruction as a species. This history makes clear that the great and urgent need of these times is transcendence. To survive, to regain power over our own lives, we must transcend the machine. We must recapture the ultimate sovereign right to choose values for ourselves. Many philosophers and poets over the last century have called for a return to non-machine values. But by seeming to preach a regression to the past they have caused us to miss the real point. Reality is not served by trying to ignore the machine. Our history shows that what we must do is assert domination over the machine, to guide it so that it works for the values of our choice. The last two hundred years have fundamentally and irrevocably altered the terms of man's existence. The price of survival is an appropriate consciousness and social order to go along with the revolution of science and technology that has already occurred. The chaos we are now experiencing is the inevitable and predictable consequence of our failure to rise to this necessity.

The new consciousness is utterly different. It seeks restoration of the non-material elements of man's existence, the elements like the natural environment and the spiritual that were passed by in the rush of material development. It seeks to transcend science and technology, to restore them to their proper place as tools of man rather than as the determinants of man's existence. It is by no means anti-technological, it does not want to break machines, but it does not want machines to run men. It makes the wholly rational assertion that machines should do the bidding of man, of man who knows and respects his own nature and the natural order of which he is a part. The new consciousness seeks new ways to live in light of what technology has made both possible and desirable. Since machines can produce enough food and shelter for all, why should not man end the antagonism derived from scarcity and base his society on love for his fellow man? If machines can take care of our material wants, why should not man develop the aesthetic and spiritual side of his nature?

Beyond the industrial era lies a new age of man. The essence of that age must be the end of the subjugation of man, the end of his subordination to the machine, and the beginning of the subjugation of the machine – the use of technology to create a still higher level of live, but one based upon values beyond the machine. The politics of controlling man become unimportant, the politics of controlling machines and organizations become the new concern of government. Economic equality and social ownership of the means of production are assumed, but they are now only a means to an end beyond. Man's religion and ethics will once again express the true realities of his way of life: solidarity with his fellow man, a genuine community representing a balanced moral-aesthetic order, and a continuing expansion of man's inner capacities.

Surely this new age is not a repudiation of, but a fulfillment of, the American dream. What were the machines for, unless to give man a new freedom to choose how he would live? What were they for, unless to expand individual freedom, and the range of human possibility? What is the central idea of America, unless each man's ability to create his own life? The dream was deferred for many generations in order to create a technology that could raise life to a higher level. It need be, it can be, delayed no longer.

We have all known the loneliness, the emptiness, the isolation of contemporary America. Our forebears came thousands of miles for the promise of a better life. Now there is a new promise. Shall we not seize it? Shall we not be pioneers once more? The breakdown of the Corporate State and the growth of radicalism would still lead nowhere, would still justify only despair, if there were not a new vision. It is the power of the vision that can turn hope into reality.

The extraordinary thing about this new consciousness is that it has emerged out of the wasteland of the Corporate State, like flowers pushing up through the concrete pavement. Whatever it touches it beautifies and renews: a freeway entrance is festooned with happy hitchhikers, the sidewalk is decorated with street people, the humorless steps of an official building are given warmth by a group of musicians. And every barrier falls before it. We have been dulled and blinded to the injustice and ugliness of slums, but it sees them as just that – injustice and ugliness – as if they had been there to see all along. We have all been persuaded that giant organizations are necessary, but it sees that they are absurd, as if the absurdity had always been obvious and apparent. We have all been induced to give up our dreams of adventure and romance in favor of the escalator of success, but it says that the escalator is a sham and the dream is real. And these things, buried, hidden, and disowned in so many of us, are shouted out loud, believed in, affirmed by a growing multitude of young people who seem too healthy, intelligent, and alive to be wholly insane, who appear, in their collective strength, capable of making it happen. For one almost convinced that it was necessary to accept ugliness and evil, that it was necessary to be a miser of dreams, it is an invitation to cry or laugh. For one who thought the world was irretrievably encased in metal and plastic and sterile stone, it seems a veritable greening of America.

From: Charles Reich, *Greening of America,* New York, Random House, 1970

Annotations

4 **to close in on** to surround gradually from all sides – 8 **San Quentin** California state prison near San Francisco – 15 **revitalization** putting new strength into – 17 **to play out** to perform – 24 **peripheral** [pəˈrifərəl] of no great importance – 31 **Corporate State** G. Staat als Machtapparat, als festgefügtes System – 42 **irrevocable** [iˈrevəkəbl] that cannot be changed once started – 44 **to go along with** to be part of – 46 **predictable** G. voraussagbar – 46 **to rise to (a necessity, challenge etc.)** to show that one can deal with this – 54 **to do s.o.'s bidding** to obey s.o.'s orders – 62 **era** [ˈiərə] G. Ära – 63 **to subjugate** to take power over s.o. – 63 **to subordinate** to put in a position of less importance – 74 **repudiation** G. Zurückweisung – 79 **to defer** [-ˈ-] to put off until a later date – 82 **forebear** ancestor – 91 **to festoon** to ornament with chains of flowers, leaves etc. – 100 **sham** piece of deceit – 100 **to disown** to refuse to accept as one's own – 105 **miser** [-ai-] G. Geizhals – 107 **irretrievable** G. unrettbar – 106 **to encase** to surround as with a case

A) Understanding the Text

1. Can you define the characteristics of what Reich calls "a great moment in history"?
2. How is the new freedom expressed in Reich's terms?
3. How does Reich view the possibility of a social revolution? Is he aiming at a revolution, or at something else?
4. What is the negative development that America has taken?
5. What is Reich's solution to end this development?
6. Reich is talking about a "new consciousness". What should it be like in his words?
7. How does the author define the relationship between man and machine?
8. What does he call the central idea of America, of the American Dream?
9. What are the major defects of contemporary America?

10. In Reich's vision, how does the new consciousness change things? Recapitulate his examples.
11. Can you sum up what he means by the term "greening of America"?

B) Interpretation and Discussion

1. Do you agree that long hair, a new way of walking, etc. can be used as metaphors of a new consciousness?
2. Do you feel oppressed by machines? Do you think machines determine man's life, or do they help to make life easier and more comfortable? Compare your view with that of Reich.
3. Do you agree that nowadays people are controlled by machines and organizations, and that it ought to be the other way round?
4. In your opinion, what are the reasons that modern society is characterized by loneliness, emptiness and isolation –
   - technology (the machine)?
   - a false consciousness?
   - economy?
   - abundance?
   - mass society, urbanization?
   - decreasing religious belief?
   - or what else?
5. Do you think it is possible to change the individual and/or society without changing its material, economic basis, as Reich suggests? Give reasons for your opinion.

C) Language Work

1. Although a German genitive construction often has an 'of' construction as its English equivalent (die Vorherrschaft *des* Marktes – the domination *of* the market) this is not always so. How, for instance, are the following ideas expressed in the text:

   Zeugen eines großen Augenblicks der Geschichte: witnesses ... a great moment ... history
   die Menschen eines sterilen Landes: the people ... a sterile land
   ein Sprecher der Armen: a spokesman ... the poor

   And what prepositions could one use here:

   in allen Städten des Landes: in the cities ... the country
   der beste Fußballer der Welt: the best soccer player ... the world
   die Krater des Mondes: the craters ... the moon

2. The following phrasal verbs all occur in the text. Put in the correct prepositions.

Before we could establish any strong defensive position the enemy closed … … us.
It is difficult to sum … his arguments in a few words.
During the winter gales the islands were cut … … the mainland.
It was a difficult job which called … a good swimmer; Janet rose … the challenge and dived into the water.
Couldn't we turn the garden shed … a garage?

Bibliography

History and Criticism

Adams, James Truslow; *The Epic of America,* Boston, 1931

Boorstin, Daniel; *The Image, or What Happened to the American Dream,* New York, 1962

Carpenter, Frederic I.; *American Literature and the Dream,* New York, 1955

Croly, Herbert; *The Promise of American Life,* New York 1909

Holbrook, Stewart; *Dreamers of the American Dream,* Garden City, N.Y., 1957

Jones, Howard Mumford; *O Strange New World,* New York, 1942

Lynn, Kenneth; *The Dream of Success: A Study of Modern American Imagination,* Boston, 1955

Noble, David M.; *The Eternal Adam and the New World Garden: The Central Myth in the American Novel Since 1830,* New York, 1968.

Ringer, Robert J.; *Restoring the American Dream,* New York, 1979

Sanford, Charles L.; *The Quest for Paradise,* Urbana, 1961

Sevareid, Eric; *You Can't Kill the Dream,* Richmond 1969

Tipple, John; *Crisis of the American Dream: A History of American Social Thought, 1920–1940,* New York, 1968

Tracy, Brian and Helms, Erwin, eds.; *American Dreams – American Nightmares,* München, 1981

Anthologies, Textbooks and Magazine Reports

Mead, Robert D., ed.; *New Promised Land: The Story of American Civilization,* New York, 1974

Madden, David, ed.; *American Dreams, American Nightmares,* Carbondale, 1970

Smith, Lew, *The American Dream,* Glenview, 1977

Schreiber, Jane L. and Elliot, Robert C., eds.; *In Search of the American Dream,* New York, 1974

Spiegel, "Traum Amerika", Artikelserie ab No 45, 3. 11. 1975

Time; "Rediscovering America", July 7, 1980

Time; "American Renewal", Feb. 23, 1981.

Primary Sources

Albee, Edward; *The American Dream,* New York, 1961
Hemingway, Ernest; *To Have and Have Not,* New York, 1937
MacLeish, Archibald; *America Was Promises,* New York, 1939
Mailer, Norman; *An American Dream,* New York, 1965
Miller, Arthur; *Death of a Salesman,* New York, 1949
Sandburg, Carl; *The People, Yes;* New York 1936
Stegner, Wallace; *The Big Rock Candy Mountain,* New York, 1943

Acknowledgements

Chapter I.
Text 1. © 1963/64/75 by the New York Times Company.
Reprinted by permission.

Chapter II.
Text 2. © 1963/64/75 by the New York Times Company.
Reprinted by permission.
Text 3. © 1963/64/75 by the New York Times Company.
Reprinted by permission.
Text 4. Reprinted by kind permission of Mr. George Mair.
Text 5. © by the New York Times Company.
Reprinted by permission.

Chapter III.
Text 2. © 1966, 1974 Scapegoat Productions Inc.
Text 4. © 1964 by The New York Times Company.
Reprinted by permission.
Text 5. © 1956, 1959 by Allen Ginsberg.
Reprinted by permission of City Lights Books.

Pictures and Illustrations

S. 8: aus: Universal Press Syndicate, Bakersfield
S. 17: Cartoon "Give me your watch . . ." aus "Punch", London
S. 33: aus: New York Times
S. 41: aus: "The New Yorker"
S. 62: Caterpillar advertisement aus "Time Magazine"
S. 68: aus: "The New Yorker"
S. 69: Marlboro advertisement

Umschlagfoto: "Penthouse"-Magazin, New York

987 654 3